WHAT IF
GOD
EXISTS?

WHAT IF
GOD
EXISTS?

JACK BLANCH

TRUSTED
BOOKS
A DIVISION OF DEEP RIVER BOOKS

ISBN-13: 978-1-63269-013-5
Library of Congress Catalog Card Number: 2004195527

Table of Contents

    The Historic Problem of Religion
    The Religious Man Is a Weak Man
        According to Many
    Doubt Should Bring Investigation
    Is the Physical or Material World the
        Only World that Exists?
    A Force That Eludes the Scientific Method
    Indications of the Existence of a
        Spiritual World

Acknowledgments

I would like to express my profound gratitude to my wife, Joann, for her companionship and support throughout this writing process. She also had a fine eye for detail in the final preparation of the manuscript. Tim Barta gave valuable comments on sentence structure and form. Pete Gerhard, who understands the mind and heart of the target audience of this book, guided me in concepts and perspective to connect with searching people of our generation. Segundo Navaza made a unique contribution by revealing insights into his life.

Foreword

I believe that at some time in our lives all of us have asked ourselves, as we observe the amazing display of nature, if God exists. Some, including myself, have pursued this question even further, looking for evidences of his existence. I only wish that in those moments I could have had at my disposal a book like this. It would have saved me a lot of searching to find satisfactory answers to my vital questions.

I have always been a voracious reader. This is the first book that I have encountered that combines clear logic with simplicity, scientific objectivity coupled with honest personal illustrations, and profound convictions with a deep respect for the reader.

This is a book written for all audiences including university level. It is rich in content and grabs you from the very beginning, creating the desire to not put it down until you have finished it. It is a book for daring and honest people who want answers to the mystery of life.

Finally, it is one of the few books that could completely change the direction of one's life.

Congratulations for the privilege you have of possessing a copy.

Dr. Pablo A. Rois Dios

Journeying Together

The granite rock canyon gorge was filled with boulders the size of a semi truck. The deep rushing water dropped from pool to pool. The distance between the two sheer granite walls of the pool was somewhere around 18-22 feet. Should I try to jump it? To fall short would mean certain death in the swirling waters. Not to jump would leave me trapped in the canyon with the embarrassing prospects of a search and rescue operation.

I was high in the Sierra Nevada of California trout fishing. I made the decision. I threw my creel over to the other side and with the fishing rod in hand took a running leap. Fear and adrenaline gave me a surge and I landed on the other side, instantly covered with sweat, with my heart racing. Wisdom doesn't come with being sixteen! I am not proud of that moment. A little less adrenaline and someone else would have been writing an obituary and this book would never exist.

Why are many of us so careless with life? With a flip of a coin or a shrug of the shoulders we dismiss some of the most important aspects of life, things critical to truly being alive, and take the ultimate risk as if life was meaningless.

This raises some questions. Does it all end with a leap that doesn't quite make it? Is there more after death? Does the question of the existence of God have any bearing on these questions and on our lives?

Recently the question of the existence of God came up in a conversation and my friend commented, "I guess it doesn't make any difference." That is the theme of this book: to consider whether or not God exists, and if he does how this would impact our lives.

Do we find it difficult to imagine anything good coming out of discussing this subject? Does guilt by association still profoundly influence us? Let me explain. In most movies and the press, what God is like is inferred from the lives of repulsive characters who claim to be guided by God. When you think of God what type of people come to your mind? Jim Jones stands out because of his fanatical followers and their mass suicide. Tele-evangelists with their fleecing of the public in the name of God are ever before us. Fanatical suicide bombers looking for eternal bliss are now often in the news. In the recent past, blowing up abortion clinics seemed to be a favorite of some religious people. Doesn't it make you wonder if God is sadistic, loves murdering people, is always angry with us? Or that he only uses fanatical, self-righteous, bigoted followers? Have you fallen for guilt by association assuming that since these people are so bad, God must be like them?

A few years ago I was living in a dictatorship that took a strong stand against drugs. At that time two American girls were sharing an apartment. One girl was caught with drugs and that afternoon both were whisked off to the airport, put on a flight to the United States and included in the "cannot return" list. Despite what we may feel about the girl on drugs, do we cry, "Foul, unjust!" for the second girl whose fault was that of being the roommate of the first girl? Have we done the same with God? Do we write him off or nullify him in our thinking because of some nuts that associate themselves with him? Should God be crying out, "Foul, unjust!"?

For others of us, maybe the idea of God is like Einstein's theory of relativity, $E=mc^2$. Both God and the formula are easy to say or write and look like they should be quite simple, but on close scrutiny they seem incomprehensible. We use the word or the formula as if we knew what we were talking about. Even the common person on the street nods his or her head in acknowledgement as if they had complete understanding.

I am working my way through a book, *The Universe in a Nutshell*, by the person people think of as a present-day Einstein, Stephen Hawking. For Einstein's formula $E=mc^2$, he explains that "E" is energy, "m" is mass and "c" is the speed of light. Included in the theory of relativity is the idea that space and time must be curved. He dedicates a chapter to theories about the shape of time. He gets my mind so twisted around that I realize I will never understand the basics of that simple little formula, $E=mc^2$.

Have you drawn a similar conclusion about God? That he is a being whom you will never be able to begin to comprehend so why try? Could it be possible he is easier to begin to comprehend than the theory of relativity? This book will investigate the possibility that God is comprehensible.

Others of you previously believed in a knowable God who hasn't "come forth with the goods" as some might say. As a result you have been disillusioned with him and have concluded he isn't what you thought he was. Your case is the more difficult one. You have "tasted" and found him bitter or lacking. You won't quickly taste again and understandably so. I more easily identify with you. When I was growing up I bit into a plastic "apple" so to speak, tasting what I thought was God but turned out not to be. Later on I bit into the real thing, God as he truly is, and got a very pleasant surprise. I don't expect you to take my word for it. But I do hope we can walk together in a journey of new discovery.

It will help us in our search to begin by doubting everything, to take nothing for granted. We will need to reason over each issue you will find in the table of contents. Questioning everything my parents or society had taught me about God was the fastest and most certain way for me to let go of mistaken assumptions and to embrace new ideas that could stand up to investigation. If you can stay with me to the end we might be able to conclude what is worth "leaping for" or which "apple" to bite.

More than Materialism

The Historic Problem of Religion

Anthropologists have noted that humanity historically has been incurably religious. It is a mystery as to why. In early times it seems people searched for things to worship such as the sun, stars, moon and earth. The Mayans worshipped a bird, the Romans called the Caesars gods, and Africans and others worshipped wooden and stone images. The Japanese worshipped their ancestors, the Jews worshipped one invisible god, and the Hindus have hundreds and hundreds of gods. Arabs worship a single god, the Christians a three-in-one god who they claim showed himself in the person of Jesus who died and returned to life. Others worship something they call Mother Earth. Some believe in an invisible and indefinable force called Mother Nature.

Under the influences of Darwin, Marx, and Lenin, much of the Western world and parts of Asia discarded the idea of a creator god. They felt they proved scientifically and philosophically that the universe has no purpose or meaning. It simply appeared, organized itself, and improved upon itself. The current atheistic scientific view is of ever-evolving life forms driven by some inexplicable force to keep improving themselves. But this life force is unable to control the medium in which it forms and develops, for the medium is expanding, dispersing, and growing colder to the theoretical point of eventually winning the battle over life. It will leave a cold, dead universe according to this world view.

For some curious reason this scientific atheistic view of the universe declares all scientists of religious cultures wrong. The Arab world, with its belief in Allah, is mistaken even though it has worthy scientists. The Jewish scientists with their belief in YHWH are mistaken. The significant world of educated scientific Hindus and Buddhists are equally mistaken. Even the significant numbers of Christian scientists in the Western world are dismissed as irrelevant and prejudiced non-thinkers. For some reason these atheistic scientists have concluded that God and science are incompatible and mutually exclusive.

These scientists and those who follow their view have judged that the spiritual world does not exist even though their scientific method and instruments are only suitable to investigate a material world.

However, as with ancient humanity, many post-modern people speak of the power of the stars to influence personal destiny. Some post-modern educated Westerners search for spirit guides with whom they expect to communicate. They say they find spiritual power and guidance in crystals and mantras. What strange thing is happening to humanity?

Out of atheistic cultures of the twentieth century, ancient religions are being reborn. In the old communist Russian Empire, Islam, Russian Orthodox, Catholicism and Protestantism are in resurgence. China and East Asia are experiencing a resurgence of Buddhism, Hinduism, and Christianity. They are not emerging because these governments have encouraged them. They are developing in a hostile and dangerous environment. It seems they are like a weed under the asphalt road that insists on emerging though paved over.

The Western scientific mind is deeply puzzled that thinking, rational people can believe in a spiritual world. How can rational people believe in a Creator when to their way of thinking, science has already proven our universe came into being by a kind of spontaneous combustion? Why is there always that niggling question lurking in the recesses of the mind, "Who or what caused the first spark?" Why is it so difficult to keep God dead?

The Religious Man Is a Weak Man According to Many

Is the reason humanity is so religious that it emotionally cannot live life without purpose or meaning? Is it so weak that it must grasp for a psychological crutch? Does it deceive itself into believing a lie because it is too painful to live with the possibility that life is meaningless?

I find two main reasons non-god people believe others believe in God. The first is they believe people live in mental darkness. Uneducated millions are religious because they don't know any better. They have not been enlightened by science. Yes, they have gone to schools to learn to read and write, but their society has kept them from comprehending the reality of scientific proof according to them.

These so called "proofs" are theories but many scientists believe they are no longer theories. They believe them to have become indisputable facts. Some would admit to a highly educated scientist proposing some alternative theory through a new piece of scientific information, but only one of their own, thus creating an exclusive club.

The second reason this group of people believes why others believe in God, or in a higher being, is because of the pain of purposelessness. It is supposed to drive them to irrational thinking, grasping at straws. They are too weak to endure the idea that life is purposeless, and for them the pain is so unbearable they create the idea of God.

One evening a group assembled in my home to discuss the possible existence of God. An interesting turn came to the debate when a God-believer accused his friend, an atheist, of being one because it was the easiest way out of the dilemma. The atheist replied with deep emotion that his atheism was almost unbearable. To live with no meaning to life and the belief that there was nothing beyond death, was agonizing to him. It should be to any of us.

Doubt Should Bring Investigation

While in college this "enlightenment," as the scientific world might call it, hit me. I had been raised to believe in Christianity and had not doubted it until I had been studying for a science degree for some time. Creation and evolution came into conflict in my mind. It was then I asked myself why I believed in Christianity. The answer came to me very clearly, in my case it was because I was taught it since childhood. I concluded this was not reason enough to believe it.

Yet what proof did I have that these new ideas from science were true? I had swallowed Christianity without thinking and I didn't want to swallow evolutionism the same way. I began a search for the truth, with a skeptical attitude toward both ideas. The truth was not easily evident for I found both religious people and atheistic scientists denying their own contradictions. Objectivity is not easily attained.

I discovered that an atheist could as easily grow up in a biased environment as a religious person, especially if he is in a university environment as a professor. The anti-god sentiment can be so strong that it becomes virtually impossible to investigate objectively the unthinkable, i.e., the existence of a power higher than higher education. Add to that the fear of disdain from fellow professors and the possible loss of job opportunity, and the motive for objectivity greatly reduces. To research against current thought, especially of peers, has always required a valiant heart. We have many examples of this in the scientific community as well as the religious. It is truly a dangerous pursuit.

It scared me when I made the decision to pursue truth no matter where it would lead. I felt my Christian family could endure my becoming an atheist or agnostic, but not becoming a Muslim. I felt if truth led me there I would be totally rejected by the people I loved most. But to be true to myself I decided with some fear that even if it led me to Islam I would follow it there. I could not believe a falsehood just to be accepted and loved. Some of you have taken this very difficult road of not following in the same religious path as your relatives and you understand my feelings.

The search for truth is not just an academic pursuit; it also has an emotional involvement. Pain is present. If you know a person in this stage of life I would appeal to you to be sensitive and compassionate as they progress in their quest.

While getting his undergraduate degree a friend of mine had a poignant conversation with his professor. His professor had dedicated his life to finding out if a worm turned left or right and why it turned that way. The student commented if that was all of the meaning he had in life he would commit suicide. In a moment of brutal honesty, the professor confessed he had tried to commit suicide but hadn't had the courage to consummate it!

Suicide is not the solution. It is an exit but it leaves enormous pain with those who remain. Let us not hurry to exit; no man seems to have found a way to return if it was a bad decision. For the sake of fairness I would like to note, however, that the Hindus believe death is a revolving door.

We have all benefited from the scientific mind. We certainly understand our astronomic, atomic, and subatomic world better. We have even profited religiously. In ages past it was a common belief that the earth rested on the back of a large tortoise. Well, we have sent men into orbit around the earth and have discovered the tortoise isn't there. We know many material mysteries still remain as we investigate the astronomic and subatomic worlds. We look forward to new discoveries of our material world.

Is the Physical or Material World the Only World That Exists?

The academic scientific world is only a small part of the world we live in and many things happen that are unexplainable by science. There is a whole series of events that cannot be evaluated by means (such as a microscope, test tube, other apparatus, or accepted scientific method) that can only evaluate a material universe.

Let me first deal with the human person. We don't seem to have grasped very well the human spirit, what motivates it, forms it, distorts it, or fulfills it. Some things leave it hopeless, empty, and lifeless, though living. You may not even believe that man has a spirit.

You may analyze yourself as an accumulation of cells united into a complex form that allows five senses to function. Each of these five senses can be studied and analyzed with normal scientific instruments. You may see yourself as no more than an animal with superior brain power (in most cases).

However, there are some elusive senses that humans experience. These are: values, morals, aesthetics and virtues. With these we move beyond the realm of the material. Values are not subject to the testing of physical instruments. They are intrinsic. No one has yet seen a scientist with a jar of values on his shelf that he has extracted from someone. What are these things that are more elusive than the subatomic quark? It seems that each person possesses his or her own packet of values, morals, aesthetics and virtues.

I am not attempting to prove mankind has a spiritual aspect to him. I do, however, want you to consider the possibility of its existence.

Why do I even bring up the subject? It leads us into the realm of the spiritual. This area is as observable as is the material universe but must be approached with a different mindset. How can we reason together about the existence of God unless there is a willingness to consider another option and to evaluate the evidence?

As we move out of the realm of academia into societies that experience spiritual phenomena on a regular basis we will encounter things quite as fascinating as space itself.

When you first begin investigating the spirit realm, the tendency is to see it as a hoax and to start searching to find where the trick is, how you are being fooled.

As in any field of endeavor there are deceivers who for financial gain, fame, or other motives, trick the gullible. A diligent search will allow us to get beyond this obstacle to reality.

A Force That Eludes Scientific Method

One day I was confronted with a force that eludes scientific proof. A friend of mine needed to drill a well and hired a well witcher or dowser to find the water. Now you may laugh and expect him to lose his money to this imposter. Using a willow branch, the dowser walked around until he came to a spot where it bent strongly downward in his hands indicating the underground flow of water. Next he took a wire and held it out over the spot. It bounced up and down strongly. It bounced 76 times and it suddenly stopped and started swinging sideways. The dowser declared that at 76 feet they would find a good stream of water.

Would you have watched closely to see how his hands manipulated the wire to make it stop and go sideways? I would have. And then you ask yourself why one bounce equals one foot, why not one meter?

Taking the financial risk, my friend then hired a well driller (a real one) to begin drilling at that spot. At 74 feet, two feet short, the drill bit hit solid rock and no water yet. Would they pay him to put on a harder bit and to drill the rock? What would you have done? They decided to have him do it and at 76 feet they hit a solid stream of water. That well continues to serve them beautifully today.

Shortly after the drilling, they told me that for some people the willow and wire work, and for others not. And with no good explanation! They offered to let me try it. I took the wire in my hand. It was a wire about as thick as a coat hanger and about 2-3 feet long. I held it tightly not knowing what to expect. To my amazement the wire strongly dipped down and bounced back as if some force was pulling it. I held it more securely so it wouldn't be pulled out of my hand. Even more amazing to me was that as I counted its bounces, at 76 it stopped. Then it started going sideways indicating it had reached the water.

I discovered that this phenomenon doesn't work with everyone. I don't know why. It is all still a mystery to me. It always worked for me. It was so interesting that often I used to take friends out to a field to demonstrate it. My friends were skeptical, as well they should have been. They watched me take a wire and hold it firmly. They observed it start dipping down with force. Then at a certain point it stopped driving downward and abruptly started swinging laterally indicating it had located the underground stream of water.

Not believing it was real, they would take the wire and try to make it do what they had just seen. That is when they discovered that this process can't be faked. If you try to make a bouncing wire stop and go sideways you discover it starts going in an elliptical circle. It is very easy to see if someone is faking it or not.

This example illustrates two things. One is that I have encountered a force I don't understand and have absolutely no explanation for although many people have theories. The other is that only my most intimate friends don't think it is a trick. In the Western culture we don't believe in supernatural and spiritual forces so we always look for the trick. In many other cultures the people recognize that spiritual forces are clearly at work and so, few would doubt the simple water-finding experience.

Indications of the Existence of a Spiritual World

This natural tendency for materialists to doubt the spiritual creates an obstacle in discovering the truth of it. People are not machines. They dislike being laughed at or scoffed. Therefore, if they suspect a person is a scoffer they will hide the information they have from the materialist.

Recently I was in South America to learn what I could from people who experienced these manifestations. I sensed reluctance on their part to talk of their experiences because they suspected I wouldn't believe them. As they began to talk about what they had experienced I noticed the side-glances they gave me to see how I was reacting. An attitude of disbelief on my part would have closed this door to me. I won't even tell you at this point what they told me because you would probably stop reading in disbelief.

Another reason materialists have not encountered much on this subject is because they are not searching for it. My life's work has been involved with people, mostly at the university. But I am always connected with the emotional and spiritual needs of people so they share this side of their lives. You may be amazed at the number of collegiates I talk with who have experienced some things that have scared them very much. I have talked to those who have had unusual experiences with ouija boards, witches, healers, etc. Things move on their own, fly through the air, etc., as if moved by an invisible being. Yes, there are those who fake things, but the real also exists.

A couple of years ago I was called to a home to help rid it of a bothering spirit. There was constant spirit activity in the home, so much that even neighbors had observed it. As a result the entire neighborhood was apprehensive. At night objects would move around the house and the front of the pictures would be turned toward the wall. They even had to get rid of all matches because the kitchen matches would ignite on their own. The husband, an officer in the Navy, was not a spiritual minded man. He was not interested in God or any of these things. He had no explanation, but wanted someone to do whatever could be done so their home would return to normal.

When I got off my flight and was introduced to him I saw he had a bandage on his forehead. He had just returned from emergency care to get stitches. He related how just a few hours before he had been sitting in his living room when things happened. The living room and the kitchen were divided by a partial wall that had three canisters for coffee, sugar, and flour sitting on it. As he was sitting on the living room couch one of the canisters flew through the air and hit him on the head necessitating his visit to the emergency room. Getting stitches in his head proved to him it was not his imagination!

I write this not to be sensational but as an example of the existence of a dimension that is not subject

to proof by scientific, materialistic methods or tools.
I hope to create a mindset that might consider the
possibility of this other dimension. Can you consider
the possibility of a spiritual being called God?

But first, let me deal with some of the reasons
that cause people to reject the idea of God.

Chapter
3

Obstacles to
Believing In God

I n the first century the Athenians had an altar
whose inscription was, "To The Unknown God."
I am writing to the person who doubts the existence of God, with the expectation that we can
think together about the possibility of a God who
is unknown to you.

But you say to me, "Why should I be interested
in this possibly existent God?"

Problems Created By the Historic Actions of Christianity

I would suppose that your encounters with the
religious world have revealed injustices, oppression,
lies, pride, hypocrisy, etc., that have caused you to
reject Christianity and God.

History confirms with abundant evidence that
those who claim to be "the people of God" have

committed great injustices. Jesus himself was in conflict with their behavior, especially when the Jews of his time said, "Abraham is our father", that is to say, "We are the people of God."

Jesus answered them, "If you were Abraham's children, then you would do the things Abraham did. As it is, you are determined to kill me, a man who has told you the truth I heard from God. Abraham did not do such things."[1]

I think we would agree that there are many hypocritical and dangerous religious people. But at the same time I would like to affirm there are also sincere and good religious people, such as Mother Teresa of Calcutta, and many others who have demonstrated exemplary characteristics we like seeing in humanity.

We need to be able to differentiate between God and those religious people who say they are from God. The church or churches are composed of humans, but God is God. In spite of human behavior, God continues to be himself. Doesn't it seem reasonable to you that God's characteristics should be very different from those of men? Although some may say they speak on his behalf, should we not draw the conclusion that the most we can expect of humanity is that they are a distant shadow of him? Mother Teresa demonstrated some characteristics of God, but she would have been the first to admit that she only demonstrated a vague semblance to him.

The pope says he speaks for God, and the church says she is a manifestation of him on the earth. The purpose of thinking together on the subject of God is to investigate and to prove what is possible to investigate. As I previously stated the attitude of this book is to begin doubting everything and then at the end to hold what we find to be true.

Following this principle then, we will put in doubt the declarations of God, Jesus Christ, the Bible, other religious books and influential religious leaders. I don't do this for the lack of respect for God, or for these people, or sacred books, or institutions, but merely to respect the rigor of investigation and objectivity. When I began my own search to understand these things, I took the position of a skeptic to avoid self-deception. I believe this position is necessary to be able to have a solid measure of confidence when we have concluded our investigation.

For Many, God Is an Undesirable Being

One of the obstacles to the desire to investigate the possibility of a God is the concept that if God does exist, he is undesirable to know. We ought to avoid him at all cost.

Once I was having a conversation with a recent acquaintance. During the course of our conversation I mentioned the name of God to this new acquaintance. To my great surprise, he screamed out on the street corner in public (very embarrassing), "I hate God. Don't speak to me about God." He continued to scream about God for two or three minutes. I just stood there, cemented to the sidewalk. What could have caused him to react so violently?

When he stopped yelling, I simply said, "Tell me what happened."

He said, "God killed my fiancée." If it were true, we would all understand and be sympathetic toward his anger and hate. Maybe there is some reason you too hate God.

It seems to be a common concept that if God exists and has such great power, he is responsible for everything, good and bad. Some believe if there is a God he kills millions with hunger and is the cause of all of the injustices on earth. He kills fiancées and others. Who would want to know a God like that? If this is your idea of God then I understand your hatred for him because he is killing your loved ones and does terrible things to humanity.

But, we must ask ourselves, is this really true? Is God responsible for all of the disasters of humanity?

Returning to the acquaintance who felt God had killed his fiancée, I asked him how God had killed her. He told me she died in a car accident! I asked him if he didn't think that the other driver, who didn't apply the brakes on his car, shouldn't be considered responsible for her death. He stood there thinking, like it was the first time he had considered that the other driver could be responsible instead of God.

Is God Responsible For All Human Behavior?

What is it that compels us to think that if God exists he is the cause of everything gone wrong? It seems to me you decide who you are going to marry, what business or employment you are going to be involved in, what you are going to do with your time, how you are going to spend your money, and a thousand other things. When your decisions turn out well, you congratulate yourself, and when things go badly, you blame God. If this is your viewpoint on life, yes, you will hate God.

I suppose what influenced this man to think God had killed his fiancée was the concept that if God is all-powerful, why didn't he stop it from happening? If there is an all-powerful God he must be really bad for letting so many innocent people suffer.

Even if there is an all-powerful God it may be that humanity is responsible for its own actions and we can go against what God desires.

I see three possible scenarios about God and man.

The First Is That God Decides Everything

He decides everything and only allows what he desires to happen. He does everything that is done. This is the extreme deterministic view. From man to insects, everything is pre-programmed. Life is then a farce. We can't actually do anything of our own free will. All that has to do with independent activity in the universe is an illusion. If this is your viewpoint, then you must be enormously frustrated. Well, maybe not, for I suppose even frustration would not be permitted. Obviously, I don't see this as the real scenario or I wouldn't encourage you to seek God because if this activity weren't pre-programmed it wouldn't occur.

There are people who hold this viewpoint. I had a friend who held this idea. I also visited an Indian tribe that held it. Both the person and the tribe have one thing in common, they are passive. They believe it is useless to try to change their circumstances or those of others. They accept injustices and leave abandoned people in need. They feel it is useless to try to change circumstances, for these circumstances are pre-ordained.

One day as I was walking along the shore of a lake, I saw a child of about two years old, floating face down in the water, motionless. The mother was near, but was enjoying the sun, resting against a large boulder with her back to the water. I shouted loudly to the mother and pointed to the water. The mother leaped up, ran into the water, grabbed her daughter and was able to start her breathing again immediately. I believe if I had done nothing to help, the child would be dead and I would share the responsibility.

I don't believe in the deterministic position for various reasons. There is too much evidence that people's actions make a difference. All of the advances in society come from people who believe they can make a difference in bettering our world. Both Christianity and Judaism admire the Ten Commandments they believe God gave through Moses. We know at least that their God isn't this way or he wouldn't have given them commandments to obey. With a totally deterministic world, commandments are useless. They imply we have control over our actions.

If God determined everything, we would not have the concept of chance. Chance is based on mathematical probabilities. If there is no probability, there is no chance. In college we study the mathematics of chance and the formulas that control them. They are operative.

The deterministic perspective denies all we have learned about choices, decision-making, and change. The reality of our daily life denies this position.

The Second Possibility Is That God Is Not Interested In the Universe

It is as if he created the world and then went on vacation or made something and then abandoned it. I must admit, on the surface, it often looks like this is what has happened. It seems that everyone just does what he wants without any intervention of a superior power. If God is here, why doesn't he do something, why doesn't he intervene? We cry out, "Help God, if you are here!" But it seems that all that we hear is the lonely echo of our own voices, and then a profound silence. I think the only possible answer to this position is if the third possibility is true.

The Third Possibility Is the Dilemma of an All-powerful God

Could it be that God is all-powerful, but that he is willing to let man live independent of him if he chooses? That he makes man responsible for his own actions but allows him to do harm to others if he prefers. That he has the option to rebel against God. This is a God who is all-powerful but who gives man a large measure of personal freedom.

This option gives man dignity and responsibility. During the dictatorship my wife and I lived under for a few years, average people would risk their lives seeking freedom of expression. Those of us who have lived all of our lives under freedom of expression fail to understand the value of what we have. If you are denied it, it becomes of paramount importance. You will risk your life to gain it. This idea of freedom has an important place in how we see God.

I find it difficult to imagine a God who would not permit me the beneficial use of my faculties. But can you imagine a God who would deny you the harmful use of your faculties? Can you imagine what it would be like if every time you stretched your arm out to steal God paralyzed that arm to keep you from stealing? Or if each time you began to plan harm to others your brain ceased to function properly so you wouldn't think wrong thoughts? Life would become a total frustration and unlivable for you. You would rebel against God as against a most oppressive dictator!

To look at it another way, how would an adolescent develop into a responsible adult if each time he or she was going to make an inadequate decision you, as a parent, annulled it? Every young adult wants to be honored and respected by being able to make his or her own decisions. By the same token, I believe God honors humanity by giving us freedom of choice. Even in our society, we let people make their own decisions, even if it means they become criminals. However, we do demand responsibility for their acts, and we bring them before our courts for their criminal activity.

So with freedom of choice comes responsibility for those choices. If the driver of the car who killed this man's fiancée was guilty of her death, he, not God, should be blamed. People are not pre-programmed robots. All of our laws, nationally and internationally, assume personal responsibility. We really don't believe we are forced to live the way God wants us to live.

One of the negative results of freedom of choice is that innocent people suffer. One afternoon in Madrid, Spain, I was going to change lines on the underground Metro System. Upon entering the train, four men grabbed me and searched all through my clothes taking all of my money! They were rapid and efficient. The train door through which I had entered was still open. As it closed they stepped out on to the walkway and the train roared off with me inside, quite a bit poorer. I stood there a minute, dazed, not even knowing they had taken all of my money, until I searched through my pockets. With freedom of action, bad things can happen both personally and nationally.

The fact that people make bad choices doesn't mean that, if God exists, he doesn't care. It simply means that he values us so highly he has given us freedom to do either good or bad, not just good.

If this is true, it may be man who has produced the bad that we experience on Planet Earth. Maybe our pride, selfishness, and harmful desires have created famines, injustices, and wars. On the other side of the coin, good people have provided food for the starving, shelter for the homeless, and peace initiatives, in place of war, doing good to their neighbor.

Maybe God Is Just a Psychological Necessity Created By the Mind of Man

A very common philosophical stance is there is no God, he is just a psychological necessity created by the mind of man. Many people and cultures have created their own gods. The Roman Caesars made themselves out to be gods in addition to the many mythical gods they worshipped. Is this a sufficient argument to deny the existence of a universal God? Does the idea that some men create their own god, prove there is no true God?

There are a lot of movies about other life forms in space. Movie producers create space monsters to entertain and frighten us. Is the fact that they create these non-existent beings evidence that no extraterrestrial beings exist? That doesn't seem reasonable to me any more than the idea that because people create gods proves there is no God. We should not let the fruitful imagination of man be an obstacle to our investigation. I assume you will be discerning enough to judge between the imaginary gods and the real God, if he exists. To believe all that people tell us is a mistake. To believe nothing we are told when there is sufficient evidence for it is also a mistake.

Faith Is a Leap In the Dark

This idea that faith is a leap in the dark is another obstacle to the concept of God, implying that faith is something blind and senseless. There are people who take blind leaps of faith. It doesn't seem to me a very wise thing to do. The mind looks for facts to hold on to. Reason is built on evidences whether it is about God or about our material world. It is a mistake to believe just to believe, or to believe because you need to, because it brings you peace, or because it makes you feel good. We need to know what we believe is true.

While flying between Madrid and San Francisco, I became acquainted with a writer who was seated across from me. During our conversation she learned that I help agnostics resolve their doubts about God.

She said, "I have a book that speaks about life after death. But everything sounds too good to me. I am concerned that the reason I would like to believe what it says is true is because I want to believe it, not because it is true." I admired her clarity of mind and I agreed with her. We don't want to deceive ourselves into believing when there is not sufficient evidence.

As I say in Chapter 2, I could not accept a faith not built on factual evidence. I don't have this mysterious ability to take a leap in the dark that some people have. Faith does not need to be a leap in the dark. It should be a step into the light.

Some Claim Science Has Proven God Does Not Exist

I highly value the sciences. My own degree is in science. This is possibly where I learned to search for concrete evidences for my decisions and beliefs. But is it true that science has proven there is no God? It seems to me, the most that the scientific community can say is that they have not been able to confirm that God exists. This is certainly understandable because their methods and instruments are designed for the material world. When the first astronauts, the Russians, orbited the earth in 1961, it was at the height of political conflict between Eastern Europe and the West. To poke fun at the West the astronauts, as they were rotating the earth, declared they had kept a careful scrutiny out for God and didn't find him. They declared to the world that God didn't exist.

Many people have tried to prove or disprove scientifically whether or not God exists. I doubt either side can be proven scientifically because of the nature of God. Jesus once said, "God is a Spirit and they that worship him must worship him in spirit and truth."[2]

We don't have instruments yet that can measure or detect spirit. There is a debate going on as to whether or not man has a spirit. All of the scientific instruments of detection are physical and limited to working with the material world and not with spirits. Farther on I will offer effects or evidences of the presence of a God spirit. But they are evidences, not proofs. To try to prove spiritual things by material methods is a losing proposition. However, you can observe or corroborate the effects of the spirit on our material, physical world.

The Question Is: Who Cares If There Is a God?

What difference does it make? Why should the subject be important to me? Let me present some reasons to you. If there exists a being who is extremely wise and has unlimited power and who has a personal interest in you, one who looks on you with enormous interest because he likes you, it could be of great importance to have him for an ally. Besides, if it turns out you have an eternal spirit, one that outlasts your body, it may be this God Spirit has thought about your eternal dwelling place and your eternal life. (Pardon the reference to this Being as "he." I don't mean to imply he is masculine, it's just a literary form.)

If this being, God, exists, it would be reasonable to assume he has his own values and lives according to them. For example, he wouldn't let you use him for egotistical reasons nor to harm others. If he is a God that is interested in humanity, he could help you resolve any difficulties with your spouse or children or employer. If he does exist, and if your life does not end with your physical death, this subject could have an enormous impact on you. He would probably have something to do with how you live out eternity. Also, imagine if he was available every day to help you in a positive way, wouldn't it be important?

Or suppose he were to put himself to work helping you in ways that you can't help yourself? Suppose he would limit himself to helping you only when you didn't have the resources, letting you do all within your power and giving you dignity and challenges in life. Suppose too you had personal issues you could not overcome, and he could enable you to conquer them, wouldn't this interest you?

Since his specialty is spirit, maybe he could provide things of the spirit such as joy, inner peace, happiness in times of difficulty, and a sense of companionship in place of loneliness.

Well, of course, all of these things are too much to hope for. He would have to be the combination of a kind father or mother, a wealthy person, a powerful king or ruler, of enormous compassion, and available to all. Of course no one like this exists, unless …..

4

Obstacles to Believing In Evolution

How can we possibly do an adequate job of presenting the idea of God without touching on evolution? Most people find a mental conflict between the idea of God and evolution. The classical Theory of Evolution as presented by Darwin proposes that all life has come into existence through an accidental occurrence of conditions conducive to forming life, and then its development occurs naturally without the presence of a supernatural force to guide its development.

Some encounter obstacles to believing in God; I, too, encounter obstacles to believing evolution in the way it is presented to us today. I would like you to consider some of the facts of science and nature that have presented insurmountable obstacles for me in believing the classical Theory of Evolution.

The Problem of the Fossil Record

One of my college courses was geology. One of the early things our professor touched on was the different rock formations of the earth. Igneous rock is the oldest layer of rock. In this rock there are no indications of life as there are no fossils. Fossils are encountered in sedimentary layers, which are on top of igneous rock where the earth is undisturbed through upheaval. Evolutionists tell us that life slowly evolved over millions of years from the simplest imaginable life forms to more complex forms. In the oldest sedimentary layers we ought to find the simplest forms of life. As we come up to newer layers we should move from finding very few fossils as life was just getting started, to more abundant and complex fossils.

Lest you think I studied in some strange, distorted Christian college, I should say here that all of my studies were in various California colleges run by the State. I received a science degree from San Jose State University.

My geology professor taught us the above theory, then proceeded to inform us that the fossil record does not support the theory. The oldest rock shows no life, and then life appears in great abundance and includes both simple and complex life forms! This paleontological (the study of fossils) fact is a worldwide phenomenon. The theory of the evolution of life our professors were teaching us was in direct conflict with the geological evidence they were teaching us. What should someone think who was trying to be logical and objective in his or her search for truth?

How could they just overlook this contradiction so basic to the very theory they believed? When I decided to search for truth, wherever it was to be found, I decided I had to be honest with myself and not embrace contradictions in my thinking.

I am still perplexed over the acceptance of these contradictions. What kind of justification can we offer for such an attitude? I suppose since the only alternative theory for the appearance and development of life is one of creation, this is "unacceptable." People are forced to ignore these contradictions in the hope that further scientific evidence will prove the conflicting evidence false.

Why can't we just accept the geological and paleontological evidence of early appearance of abundant and varied life forms and at least consider another theory, for example of creation, as a possible alternative? At least for me, seeing the evidence and the contradiction, I couldn't just swallow the theory of evolution. I needed to hold it with an open hand to see if it would prove out. I couldn't make the required leap of faith.

Then later, I began to discover this was a problem also for many scientists. The Harvard paleontologist, Stephan Jay Gould, also had a problem with the fact that the fossil record does not support the theory of gradual transition or development of life forms.[3]

The Problem of Biased Selectivity of Data

As I continued my investigation of evolution I discovered an intentional selectivity of data that supported the theory of the origin of life and the exclusion of contradictory evidence. I became aware of various geological discoveries, and information from other branches of science, that contradicted existing theories. Somehow this information never finds its way into textbooks for people to consider. It seems to me that scientists should include, along with their preferred theory, evidence that conflicts with it so that people can see and evaluate for themselves. But the fact is, information is being withheld or not reported to the extent that other scientists often are unaware of this information. Part of the problem is that some publishers are not accepting contradictory information. We need a just and equal treatment of scientific discoveries. It doesn't speak well for the scientific community or for publishers, to withhold information just because they don't like it. I suppose withholding conflicting information is not intentional, but it certainly impedes objective investigation of the origin of life.

I admire the honesty of physicist H. S. Lipson at the University of Manchester Institute of Science and Technology and a Fellow of the Royal Society, who states, "I have always been slightly suspicious of the theory of evolution because of its ability to account for any property of living beings (the long neck of the giraffe, for example). I have therefore tried to see whether biological discoveries over the last 30 years or so fit in with Darwin's theory. I do not think that they do... I think, however, that we must go further than this and admit that the only acceptable explanation is creation. I know that this is anathema to physicists, as indeed it is to me, but we must not reject a theory that we do not like if the experimental evidence supports it."[4]

The Problem of the Improbability of Spontaneous Evolution

With the scientific advances over the past 10 years the concept of spontaneous evolution becomes increasingly remote. According to the present theory of evolution, given enough time and some favorable conditions, life will occur and evolve upwards. This sounds reasonable until we begin to take a scientific view of how probable this could be.

James F. Coppedge in his book *Evolution: Possible or Impossible?* investigates these ideas. Also John Ankerberg and John Weldon take up the issue in *Darwin's Leap of Faith.*

> Consider that the smallest *theoretical* cell is made up of 239 proteins. Further, at least 124 different types of proteins are needed for the cell to become a living thing. But the simplest *known* self-reproducing organism is the H^{39} strain of PPLO (mycoplasma) containing 625 proteins with an average of 400 amino acids in each protein.

> Yet the probability of the occurrence of the smallest *theoretical* life is only one chance in $10^{119,879}$

and the years required for it to evolve would be $10^{119,831}$ times the assumed age of the earth!

"The probability of this smallest theoretical cell of 239 proteins evolving without the needed 124 different types of proteins to make up a living cell, i.e., the chance of evolving this 'helpless group of *non-living* molecules' in over 500 billion years is one chance in $10^{119,701}$ and according to Coppedge, the probability of evolving a single protein molecule over 5 billion years is estimated at one chance in 10^{161}. This allows some 14 concessions to help it along which would not actually be present during evolution. Again, there is *no* chance.[5]

When we consider the theory of spontaneous formation of life we use the word "chance" because to use the word "design" we would be implying a creator. When we consider "chance" we enter into the mathematics discipline of probabilities which I have just been citing. Many scientists think with infinite time anything is possible. It is as if they think that with sufficient time even the most improbable will come to pass. Possibly they have not paused to consider the implications in this leap of faith.

Maybe, you as a reader haven't found mathematics to be your "strong suit." If not, I would like to give you an idea of the immensity of these numbers we have been talking about and of the improbability of the above mentioned cell and protein formation happening by chance.

It is calculated that the number of atoms in the universe is 10^{70}. If a natural process has this probability of occurring, the probability of it not happening is so overwhelming that you would discount it from happening at all. Let me illustrate this.

Right now you are reading this book. Lift up your eyes and look around you. Do you see a piece of furniture, or a wall, or a chair? How many atoms do you think are in the item you see, a thousand, millions, or billions? It is hard to even imagine how many isn't it?

Now let's paint *one* of these millions or billions of atoms red. Assuming you could touch one of these atoms, with your eyes closed, could you touch the red one on the *first* try? Your practical experience of probabilities would probably lead you to say, no. Now extend out your mind. Think not just of the furniture but of the whole earth, then the sun, then all of the stars. Would you have some hope of touching the one red atom in the entire universe on the first try with your eyes blindfolded? That is the meaning of the probability of 10^{70}! We are reaching for absurdity.

Let's continue trying to understand the implications of these exponential numbers. If 10^{70} is the number of atoms in the universe, 10^{71} means 10 times more, so if this number was the probability of finding that red atom blindfolded, it would mean that we would have to choose it out of 10 universes the size of ours! Make the number 10^{72} and we would have to choose from 100 universes.

Wouldn't you say this is so improbable that we would consider it impossible? James Coppedge has told us that the probability of the chance formation of one protein molecule is 10^{161}. When we grasp the meaning of these enormous numbers we realize the possibility of it occurring becomes unimaginable!

Now many scientists say that with unlimited time this could have occurred. The problem is that they themselves have said there isn't unlimited time. The latest calculations of evolutionists is that the entire universe is only about 15 billion years old and that the earth, where life is supposed to have been spontaneously formed, is only about 5 billion years old.

According to Emil Borel, one of the foremost world experts in calculating probabilities, beyond 10^{50} things *never* happen. There no longer exists "probability." The probability necessary for the spontaneous formation of one protein molecule is millions of times greater than Borel's limit. Serious scientists ought also to accept the science of the laws of mathematical probabilities. It is a science that any beginning math student in college must study.

The Problem of the Simultaneous Development of All of the Necessary Parts

Progressing from the simplest organisms to the more complicated, the leaps of faith for sustaining the evolutionary origin of life grow exponentially. All of the organisms, from the simplest to the most complex, cannot function unless all of the components are present and functioning. For all of the parts to have developed simultaneously and achieve functionality by evolution staggers the mind.

Let's look at a simple organism, the cilium. "A cilium is a structure that beats like a whip and looks like a hair. Cells use them for movement and cleansing. A cilium basically consists of many fibers coated with membranes. The cilium illustrates what is true for virtually every living complex entity: *all* its component parts must be present for it to function at all! Therefore, it could never have evolved piecemeal. For example, the cilium *requires* microtubules, a motor, and other things simply to perform one of its major functions, ciliary motion. Professor Michael Behe, associate professor of biochemistry, Lehigh University, points out that science cannot even explain how something as simple as the cilium evolved."[6]

Let's take the example of the feather of a bird. It is either the design of a master designer or it is a fabulous miracle of evolution. The aerodynamic principles of its design are complicated and fascinating. It has many complex components and if one of them were missing the feather would not be functional and the bird could not fly. If evolution is true, birds would have had to pass millions of years waiting for the final development of all of the components to be able to fly. Meanwhile, what was developing would have been a tremendous impediment to its normal existence making it an easy prey to predators, and survival impossible.

It forces me to ask the question, why would useless components develop that would only be useful millions of years later? Does evolution have a mind that designs and knows ahead of time what it is planning to design? Scientists, without saying it, attribute to evolution an amazing intelligence of principles of aerodynamics and a host of other principles. What gives them the right to attribute amazing intelligence to "chance?" I have no ability to make the leap of faith they ask of me. Consider further evidence that contradicts this way of thinking.

Among millions of examples I would like to have you consider the bombardier beetle and the necessity of all of its components developing simultaneously.

> The bombardier beetle is a small insect that is armed with an impressive defense system. Whenever threatened by an enemy attack, this spirited little beetle blasts irritating and odious gases, which are at 212° F, out from two tailpipes right into the unfortunate face of the would-be-aggressor.

> Herman Schildknecht, a German chemist, learned that the beetle makes his explosive by mixing together two very dangerous chemicals (hydroquinone and hydrogen peroxide). In addition to these two chemicals, this clever little beetle adds another type of chemical known as an

"inhibitor." The inhibitor prevents the chemicals from blowing up and enables the beetle to store the chemicals indefinitely.

Whenever the beetle is approached by a predator, he squirts the stored chemicals into the two combustion tubes, and at precisely the right moment he adds another chemical (an anti-inhibitor). This knocks out the inhibitor, and a violent explosion occurs right in the face of the poor attacker.

According to evolutionary "thinking" there must have been thousands of generations of beetles improperly mixing these hazardous chemicals in fatal evolutionary experiments, blowing themselves to pieces."[7]

Darwin stated that some human organs, such as the eye, were so complex that it would stagger the imagination of almost anyone to believe they were formed according to his theory. I think we can confidently say that, over 125 years ago when Darwin lived, they didn't know the half of the complexity of these organs as we do in the 21st century, and we are still discovering!

I find it more reasonable to attribute this amazing design ability to an intelligent being capable of design and planning, than to a mindless evolutionary process. I find it impossible to believe that evolution has the capacity to plan for the future and to provide for the future needs of living things.

The Problem of the Complexity of the DNA

Darwin was unaware of the existence of the molecular world and of its complexity. DNA was discovered in the second half of the twentieth century. DNA is in each cell and carries the code for the complete construction of a being, how to construct it, and when to begin construction in each phase.

> In the human body, DNA "programs" all characteristics such as hair, skin, eyes, and height. DNA determines the arrangement for 206 bones, 600 muscles, 10,000 auditory nerve fibers, 2 million optic nerve fibers, 100 billion nerve cells, 400 billion feet of blood vessels and capillaries, and so on."[8]

> If we think of the cell as being analogous to a factory, then the proteins can be thought of as analogous to the machines on the factory floor which carry out individually or in groups all the essential activities on which the life of the cell depends."[9] ... Although proteins are amazingly versatile and carry out all manner of diverse biochemical functions they are incapable of assembling themselves without the assistance of another very important class of molecules—the nucleic acids. To return again to the analogy of the factory, while the proteins can be thought of as the working elements of a factory, the nucleic acid molecules can be thought of as playing the role of library or memory bank containing all the information necessary for the construction

of all the various machines (proteins) on the factory floor. More specifically, we can think of the nucleic acids as a series of blueprints, each one containing the specifications for the construction of a particular protein in the cell.

There are two types of nucleic acids, DNA and RNA. DNA is only found in the nucleus of the cell, equivalent to the head office of the factory, and contains the master blueprints. RNA molecules perform the fundamental task of carrying the information stored in DNA to all the various parts of the cell where the manufacture of a particular protein is proceeding. In terms of our analogy we can think of RNA molecules as photocopies of the master blueprint (DNA) which are carried to the factory floor where the technicians and engineers convert the abstract information of the blueprint (RNA) into the concrete form of the machine (protein).[10]

To sum it up: every single cell carries in the DNA instructions for the construction of the entire human body (or any living organism). It gives the order in which each item should be constructed, that is, what should develop first and what second, then the timetable for each part. For example, puberty is timed by the DNA to occur at just the right period in a human. If a female were to enter puberty at age 2, it would be far too early. By the same token if she were to enter puberty at age 70, it would be too late to have children and the human race would cease to exist. All of this not only requires a Designer, it also requires a lot more intelligence than man has.

We have difficulty understanding its function, much less to be able to design it.

Are you capable of thinking that such a complicated system could have formed by pure chance? Personally I am not capable of taking this step. Am I too pragmatic?

Increasingly scientists are coming to the same conclusion. Just recently on the news it was stated that Dr. Anthony Flew, a noted British philosopher and formerly a staunch atheist, now in his 80's, has decided that Intelligent Design evidence is so strong that he now has embraced the conclusion that there must be a Designer, God.

I want to suggest three books for the reader who would like to dig more deeply into this topic:

> The Collapse of Evolution, Scott M. Huse, Published by Baker Books, 1997, http://www. bakerbooks,com.
> Evolution: A Theory in Crisis, Michael Denton, Adler and Adler, Publishers, Inc., 1986.
> Darwin's Leap of Faith, John Ankerberg and John Weldon, Harvest House Publishers, 1998.

These have been some of my obstacles to believing in the theory of evolution. I hope that they have been sufficiently reasonable to permit a discussion of God without thinking that the idea is absurd. There are grounds to doubt Darwinism and also reasons to think that God could exist. In the following chapters we will consider the evidences of the existence of God and reasons why the subject could be important for you.

Chapter 5

The Book That Was Approximately 2,000 Years In The Making

For the moment, let's suppose that God exists. If he is a being who doesn't want to be known or discovered, he could easily hide himself so he could never be discovered. I am going to suppose he wants to be discovered and known. Without this supposition this book would have no reason to be written.

In the search for God I also suppose that he is far greater than mankind and should have supernatural powers. Do you agree with me? What would God be if he only had the natural powers that we have? We are beings that must obey the natural laws of the universe. Our existence depends on living within the limits they impose upon us.

If there is a God, I can only imagine him as a being with supernatural powers that are part of his

51

normal existence and experience. If he is eternal, he
is not subject to the things that cause us death. If he
can live in an "atmosphere" that we consider much
more hostile to life, such as outer space, and if his
habitat is extremely different, then things he would
do would seem to us supernatural. Isn't that true?
Then it should seem reasonable to you if I mention
powers way beyond the normal sphere of mankind
when talking about him. We can't speak about God
without bringing into view the miraculous from our
viewpoint.

I have read a book that claims to proceed from
God, so that we might know him and at the same
time understand the purpose of our existence. It is
a book that took almost 2,000 years to write. It is
known as the Bible or the Sacred Scriptures, depend-
ing on whom you talk to. Possibly you consider it a
fairy tale because of its stories of the supernatural.
I doubted it and had to put it to the test. I did not
want to believe it without good evidence for fear that
after believing it I would find that I was mistaken
and would have to back-pedal in many issues.

What Is the Bible?

It is like a miniature library because it contains
66 books or writings. The first part begins with the
writings of Moses who lived about 1500 B.C. It deals
with issues and people up until about 350 B.C., a
period of about 1,150 years. The second part begins

just before the birth of Jesus, talks about him and his followers, and ends about 98 A.D.

A common phrase of the Bible is, "God said." It claims to be the communication of God to mankind.

It is not an enchanted book, but it is similar to that in many aspects. You have probably seen some movie about magic, where there is an enchanted book of witches that is filled with curses. If you knew the magic words or incantations, you could invoke the curses. In a way of speaking, it might be considered a living book.

This book of which I speak, the Bible, is filled with blessings instead of curses. It also speaks about what God is like. But to the normal reader it doesn't open itself. It is a book that is curiously alive. A normal book gives up its ideas to an inquiring mind. This book does not open its ideas to the curious mind but rather opens to the sincere heart that seeks to understand God.

You may say, "You are feeding me another fairy tale." But I must tell you the things as they are, not as we would like them to be. It claims to represent the thoughts of a supernatural being and to be a supernatural book.

You might try reading it just as you would read a normal book, and then become angry because you can't understand it. You might even tear out pages in frustration and throw them in the garbage, and find that the Author won't even protest. But if you open it with respect and have an open mind and heart you will discover its treasures. This book is unique in that it opens its treasures to the heart. The right attitude is important to begin to understand God.

We must ask ourselves, as I did, why should we think that this book is the communication of a supernatural being? How should we go about deciding if it is something to throw away or something to believe? First I would say, though you may doubt it, read it with respect for it may turn out to be true.

Suppose you were going to discuss the subject of lions but you had never seen one in person. If there were a zoo nearby where you could personally observe them, the wisest thing would be to make a visit and get firsthand information. It is the same with the Bible. Rather than just talk around what you may not have observed firsthand, go to a bookstore or a library and get a Bible. Look at it yourself. Why be content with secondhand information?

Is the Bible History or a Fairy Tale?

Moses was born about 1520 B.C. Did writing exist during this time? In October of 2000 my wife and I visited Greece. An official tourist guide confidently told our group that the Greek language had the first existing alphabet and it originated in 700 B.C. This comment would naturally carry much weight since the tourist guide was authorized by the Greek government.

To the average person she gave the impression that writing did not exist prior to 700 B.C., that prior to that date everything was recorded graphically or in hieroglyphics. That would mean the events of Moses would have had to be passed on orally or by hieroglyphics for 700 years without change, which we would find difficult to accept.

Archaeology confirms the existence of writing during the period of the life of Moses, the author of the first five books of the Bible. In 1968 an ancient library containing 1,600 written tablets was discovered in Ebla, northern Syria. The tablets were written prior to its destruction in 2250 B.C.

> Another significant outcome of the Ebla discovery delivered a crushing blow to the documentary supposition that Moses could not have written the Pentateuch (*the first five books of the Bible*) because writing was nonexistent in his day. The proponents of the documentary hypothesis have claimed that the period described in the Mosaic narrative (1400 B.C., a thousand years after the Ebla kingdom) was prior to all knowledge of writing. But the findings from Ebla demonstrate that a thousand years before Moses, laws, customs, and events were recorded in writing in the same area of the world in which Moses and the patriarchs lived."[11]

Does Archaeology Confirm the Places and Cities Mentioned in the Old Testament?

In Moses' first book, Genesis, chapter 14 was in historical doubt because the five cities mentioned in verse 8, "Then the king of **Sodom**, the king of

Gomorrah, the king of **Admah**, the king of **Zeboiim** and the king of **Bela** (that is, Zoar) marched out and drew up their battle lines in the Valley of Siddim."[12] The Valley of Siddim was in the Jordan Valley in the area of the Dead Sea. Archeology had not as yet uncovered these cities. But in the archeological find of the tables of Ebla, they found tablets that spoke of these five cities, and in exactly the same order, now confirming the account of Moses.

During the period of 1900 to 1960 there was a lot of criticism of the Bible because of "supposed" historical errors. During the period of approximately 1945 to 1965 there were multiple excavations of biblical sites. Using the Bible as a guide, a number of cities were discovered by excavation in the places indicated by the Bible in its historical writings. They have confirmed the existence of cities and peoples who were previously undiscovered. Also data has been discovered confirming strange circumstances that were in question. One example among many is that of the Hittites.

In a book of the Bible entitled First Kings (a record of the kings of Israel), we read, "They imported a chariot from Egypt for six hundred shekels of silver, and a horse for a hundred and fifty. They also exported them to all the kings of the Hittites and of the Arameans."[13]

They have uncovered other records of the renting of chariots from Egypt during this period. However, up until the decade of 1920 there had been no evidence of the existence of the Hittites. This created a lot of doubt about the Bible, especially since the Bible referred to them as an important people. In recent years, because of numerous archaeological discoveries, the existence of this people has become well documented. There are even entire books written describing the Hittite people and their empire.

Year after year confirmation of cities and peoples is happening through excavations. We can trust the biblical historical record of the region. But the questions remains, can we trust the details?

Let me give just a few examples to also set this issue at rest.

In the biblical record of the times of Israel's first king, Saul, and of the second king, David, the subject of the sling comes up. Today we know the sling as a toy thing that would be absurd to use as a battle instrument. The Bible mentions the men of Gibeah, the town that later became the fortress of King Saul. "At once the Benjamites mobilized twenty-six thousand swordsmen from their towns, in addition to seven hundred chosen men from those living in Gibeah. Among all these soldiers were seven hundred chosen men who were left-handed, each of whom could sling a stone at a hair and not miss."[14]

Gibeah has been excavated and in the process it was discovered that the sling was an important instrument of war, confirming the above account.

Another supposed biblical error has to do with the account of Israel's first king, Saul.

"Upon Saul's death, Samuel tells us that his armor was put in the temple of Ashtaroth (a

Canaanite fertility goddess) at Bet She'an, while Chronicles (a book of the Old Testament) records that his head was put in the temple of Dagon, the Philistine corn god. This was thought to be an error because it seemed unlikely that enemy people would have temples in the same place at the same time. However, excavations have found two temples at this site that are separated by a hallway: one for Dagon, the other for Ashtaroth. It appears that the Philistines had adopted the Canaanite goddess.

One of the key accomplishments of David's reign was the capture of Jerusalem. Problematic in the Scripture account was that the Israelites entered the city by way of a tunnel that led to the Pool of Siloam. However, that pool was thought to be outside the city walls at that time. Excavations in the 1960's finally revealed that the wall did indeed extend well past the pool."[15]

These are few among the many examples of historical confirmation of the Bible by archaeology.

How Can We Have Confidence in a Book Translated so many Times? Hasn't It Been Changed by These Translations?

Almost all of the people with whom I talk that have a sparse knowledge of the Bible think it has lost its original text through many successive translations. They will ask who knows what the original was like. It is because they are uninformed of how the Bible is translated. It is an important issue that requires a solid answer.

The Bible comes in two sections, the Old Testament and the New Testament. The Old Testament deals with events that occurred prior to the birth of Jesus and the New Testament deals with Jesus and his Apostles and their writings. Antique documents exist for both parts.

These antique documents are the source for each succeeding translation. For the most part the original languages of the Old Testament were Hebrew and Chaldean and for the New Testament they were Aramaic (local language of Palestine) and Greek.

As the Old and New Testaments are translated from one language to another the antique documents are used, always returning to the originals.

I would like to note that there have been some translations over the years that were not done this way. One example is the use of Saint Jerome's (347 A.D. to 420 A.D.) translation into Latin called the Vulgate. Later, out of a great appreciation for Latin, other translations were made from this one instead of returning to translate directly from the original languages. However in the fifteenth and sixteenth centuries they corrected this mistake and began once again to make translations directly from the original languages. The current translations are done correctly.

Rather than more translations corrupting the Bible, they actually are important to preserve the original ideas. Language is a living vibrant thing.

It is constantly changing. Every two or three
generations a new translation needs to be made to
preserve the true sense of the literature.

In the English language, the favorite Bible
Protestants most used was translated in England in
1611 and was such a masterpiece that people were
reluctant to bring it up to date. As a result it became
more and more difficult to understand. Pastors
would always be explaining the meanings of words
from about 400 years ago so the congregations could
understand. Our most accurate translations now in
English are just 10 to 20 years old.

I would like to turn now to the consideration
of the oldest documents we have so you are not left
with a mistaken impression. You will then understand the degree of authenticity of the present day
Bibles.

No original document has been preserved. For
example, we don't have the original five books that
Moses wrote 3,500 years ago. What we have are
copies of the original. This brings up the question
of their validity.

Since these were documents considered "sacred"
by the Jews, they took special measures to preserve
their accuracy. In the following you will see the
almost exaggerated measures they took to preserve
accuracy for future generations. They went to great
lengths to make sure that a copy was an exact copy
of the prior copy. I would like to remind you that
up until the 16th century when the printing press
was invented, all books were written by hand, one

by one, and were called manuscripts. The following is how the Talmudists did their transcribing.

(1) A synagogue roll must be written on the skins of clean animals, (2) prepared for the particular use of the synagogue by a Jew. (3) These must be fastened together with strings taken from clean animals. (4) Every skin must contain a certain number of columns, equal throughout the entire codex. (5) The length of each column must not extend over less than 48 or more than 60 lines, and the breadth must consist of thirty letters. (6) The whole copy must be first-lined; and if three words be written without a line, it is worthless. (7) The ink should be black, neither red, green, nor any other color, and be prepared according to a definite recipe. (8) An authentic copy must be the exemplar, from which the transcriber ought not in the least deviate. (9) No word or letter, not even a yod, must be written from memory, the scribe not having looked at the codex before him... (10) Between every consonant the space of a hair or thread must intervene; (11) between every new parashah, or section, the breadth of nine consonants, (12) between every book, three lines. (13) The fifth book of Moses must terminate exactly with a line; but the rest need not do so. (14) Besides this, the copyist must sit in full Jewish dress, (15) wash his whole body, (16) not begin to write the name of God with a pen newly dipped in ink, (17) and should a king address him while writing that name he must take no notice of him.[16]

Frederic Kenyon, in *Our Bible and the Ancient Manuscripts*, expands on the above concerning the destruction of older copies: "The same extreme care which was devoted to the transcription of manuscripts is also at the bottom of the disappearance of the earlier copies. When a manuscript had been copied with the exactitude prescribed by the Talmud, and had been duly verified, it was accepted as authentic and regarded as being of equal value with any other copy. If all were equally correct, age gave no advantage to a manuscript; on the contrary age was a positive disadvantage, since a manuscript was liable to become defaced or damaged in the lapse of time. A damaged or imperfect copy was at once condemned as unfit for use."[17]

The fact that we have Old Testament manuscripts no older than the tenth century is positive when we realize the care they made not to let unreadable or worn out manuscripts exist. Just to be sure that they really did do an excellent job in preserving the original writings, it would be helpful to corroborate this in some way. Fortunately, we have this corroboration in the discovery of documents that existed hidden for 1000 years prior to the tenth century, that is, from approximately 100 B.C., the Dead Sea Scrolls.

The story of this discovery is one of the most fascinating tales of modern times. In February or March of 1947 a Bedouin shepherd boy named Muhammad was searching for a lost goat. He tossed a stone into a hole in a cliff on the west

side of the Dead Sea, about eight miles south of
Jericho. To his surprise he heard the sound of
shattering pottery. Investigating, he discovered
an amazing sight. On the floor of the cave were
several large jars containing leather scrolls,
wrapped in linen cloth. Because the jars were
carefully sealed, the scrolls had been preserved in
excellent condition for nearly 1,900 years. (They
were evidently placed there in 68 A.D.[18]

The Importance of the Dead Sea Scrolls

The oldest complete Hebrew manuscripts we
possessed before the Dead Sea Scrolls were from
A.D. 900 on. How could we be sure of their accurate transmission since before the time of Christ
in the first century A.D.? Thanks to archaeology
and the Dead Sea Scrolls, we now know. One of
the scrolls in the Dead Sea caves was a complete
manuscript of the Hebrew text of Isaiah. It is
dated by paleographers around 125 B.C. This
manuscript is more than one thousand years
older than any manuscript we previously possessed.

The significance of this discovery has to do with
the detailed closeness of the Isaiah scroll (125
B.C.) to the Masoretic Text of Isaiah (900 A.D.) one
thousand years later. It demonstrates the unusual
accuracy of the copyists of the Scripture over a
thousand year period.[19]

The New Testament was not written under the Jewish system. Most of the New Testament was written by Christian Jews who were followers of Jesus. They did not follow the customs of the Talmudists (Jews) by destroying the manuscripts after copying them. We possess thousands of copies of books of the New Testament that were written about 200 years after the original works. There also exist a number of fragments dated to just a few years after the original writings which enable us to verify the accuracy of the documents we now have.

The oldest writings of the New Testament, the Gospels, record the life and teachings of Jesus Christ. Jesus died about 30 A.D. and the first Gospels were written 15-25 years after his death by eyewitnesses of his life.

The Gospel of John was written later than the first three, probably about 94 A.D. by John himself. There exist Roman and Greek government documents that declare that the Roman emperor Domitian exiled John, the apostle of Jesus, in the year 94 A.D., to the island of Patmos, part of modern day Greece. These records establish that John was living posterior to the writing of his Gospel.

There is in the John Ryland's Library of Manchester, England, a fragment of the Gospel of John that was discovered in Alexandria, Egypt, that is dated at 130 A.D.

There exists a great number of New Testament manuscripts dated from 250 A.D. and prior. This

number is overwhelming compared to the number
of old manuscripts we have of the ancient classics.

> As a result, the fidelity of the New Testament
> text rests on a multitude of manuscript evi-
> dence. Counting Greek copies alone, the New
> Testament is preserved in some 5,656 partial and
> complete manuscript portions that were copied
> by hand from the second through the fifteenth
> centuries.[20]

> There are now more than 5,686 known Greek
> manuscripts of the New Testament. Add over
> 10,000 Latin Vulgate and at least 9,300 other
> early versions (MMS), and we have close to, if
> not more than 25,000 manuscript copies of por-
> tions of the New Testament in existence today.
> No other document of antiquity even begins to
> approach such numbers and attestation. In com-
> parison, Homer's Iliad is second, with only 643
> manuscripts that still survive. The first complete
> preserved text of Homer dates from the thirteenth
> century.[21]

> Sir Frederic G. Kenyon, who was the director and
> principal librarian of the British Museum and sec-
> ond to none in authority for issuing statements
> about MSS (*manuscripts*), states that, 'besides
> number, the manuscripts of the New Testament
> differ from those of the classical authors … In
> no other case is the interval of time between
> the composition of the book and the date of the
> earliest extant manuscripts as short as in that
> of the New Testament. The books of the New

Testament were written in the latter part of the first century; the earliest extant manuscripts (trifling scraps excepted) are of the fourth century—say from 250 to 300 years later. This may sound a considerable interval, but it is nothing to that which parts most of the great classical authors from their earliest manuscripts.[22]

For *Caesar's Gaelic Wars* (composed between 58 and 50 B.C.) there are several extant MSS, but only nine or ten are good, and the oldest is some 900 years later than Caesar's day. Of the 142 books of the Roman history of Livy (59 B.C.-17 A.D.), only 35 survive; these are known to us from not more than 20 MSS of any consequence, only one of which, and that containing fragments of Books III-VI, is as old as the fourth century.[23]

To sum it up, the content of both the Old and New Testaments is trustworthy as a document that reflects what was originally written. Archeological discoveries substantiate a significant number of people, places, events, and details of the Bible. Each new discovery concerning biblical history substantiates, not contradicts, this book.

Archeology was what convinced me I should read the Bible as a historical book rather than as a fairy tale.

Because of archeology we affirm the Bible is worthy to be considered an historical account of what is written. However, archeology has its limits. It cannot affirm whether or not the Bible is from God, as it claims, or even if the ideas it espouses are correct.

It is, however, a book that lends itself to investigation and affirmation. If the book is from God, it should show evidences that it has a divine imprint. One of the indicators that we should consider is that it is written from God's viewpoint and not from the human viewpoint. It often says, "God says," and at times quotes God directly speaking to someone. It describes scenes of God's dwelling place, heaven. Since God claims to be eternal, it speaks of events prior to human history along with future events. It's as if it has no limits to its themes.

Since it seems to be a book written to mankind to eliminate doubt as to what God is like, it speaks of his characteristics and thoughts. It tells us what God thinks of man, and in certain parts, you can discover what he thinks about you personally. There will be pages, which when read you will affirm, "That's what I am like." It is a historical book, very objective, but at the same time highly personal.

Part of the reason God says he is trying to communicate with us is to help guide us in living this life and to guide us to where we will spend eternity. It does not limit itself to advising us how to live; it also offers a solution for how to become transformed and how to find the wherewithal to live a better life. God doesn't just give standards; he also offers help to live by them. Personally I read it to find guidance when I am confused, help when I find I'm in need of it, and

communication with God when people all around
me are saying, "God, where are you?"

I don't know if you would dare to do this or
not, but you might try speaking to God and saying,
"God, I don't know if you exist or not, but if you do
exist, use this book to reveal yourself to me and to
speak to me." If he is really out there somewhere,
he might respond.

In the following chapter I will present to you
what I feel is the easiest way to discover if God
exists.

Chapter

6

Who Was That Man?

I t is possible the solution to the existence of God is not resolved by a debate over his existence, but in a more oblique investigation of the authentic Jesus. You might ask how this can be? How can we resolve the dilemma by looking at a man? Because this man made the astounding claim to be God come to earth in the form of a human. A reccurring theme to the life of Jesus is that God has clothed himself with humanity in the person of Jesus so that we could more easily know and understand him. You will probably say, "Impossible." I just ask you to reserve your judgement for a bit while I present some very interesting evidence for this thesis.

What Did the Jewish Leaders at the Time of Jesus Think of Him? What Did They Understand Jesus to Be Saying About Himself?

These religious leaders were trying to kill him. Why? Let's listen in on some conversation recorded between Jesus and those leaders.

Again the Jews picked up stones to stone him, but Jesus said to them, "I have shown you many great miracles from the Father. For which of these do you stone me?"

"We are not stoning you for any of these," replied the Jews, "but for blasphemy, because you, a mere man, claim to be God."[24]

Stoning at that time was how the death sentence was executed for blasphemers.

At a prior occasion it was recorded, "For this reason the Jews tried all the harder to kill him; not only was he breaking the Sabbath, but he was even calling God his own Father, making himself equal with God."[25]

They did not kill him just because he was a prophet, or a messenger from God. They did it because they were terribly offended he would claim to be God, or equal with God, which is the same thing.

But What Was Foretold in Their Writings about Their Messiah for Whom They Were Waiting?

At Christmas time people celebrate the birth of Jesus in Bethlehem, without being aware of the explanation of who this person was. When the mortal enemy of Jesus, King Herod, tried to locate the pretender to his throne, whom rumor had it had just been born, the New Testament records,

> After Jesus was born in Bethlehem in Judea, during the time of King Herod, Magi from the east came to Jerusalem and asked, "Where is the one who has been born king of the Jews? We saw his star in the east and have come to worship him."

> When King Herod heard this he was disturbed, and all Jerusalem with him. When he had called together all the people's chief priests and teachers of the law, he asked them where the Christ was to be born. "In Bethlehem in Judea," they replied ... [26]

Where did they get this idea? They got their information from one of the books of the Old Testament where it is recorded that an eternal being would be their child king.

"But as for you, Bethlehem Ephrathah, too little to be among the clans of Judah, from you One will go forth for Me to be ruler in Israel. His goings forth are from long ago, from the days of eternity."[27]

It is not necessary at this point that you believe the Old Testament, simply that you understand what was written about Jesus before he was born.

It has been substantiated that Isaiah was a historic person (some believe there were two different Isaiahs). He wrote his book during the reigns of King Uzziah and King Manasses, that is, between 750 b.c. – 696 b.c. Let's listen to what he wrote about the Messiah or the Christ (the Greek translation of the Hebrew word Messiah).

"Therefore the Lord himself will give you a sign: The virgin will be with child and will give birth to a son, and will call him Immanuel."[28]

Immanuel is a Hebrew word whose translation is, "God with us."

In another place Isaiah wrote, "For to us a child is born, to us a son is given, and the government will be on his shoulders. And he will be called Wonderful Counselor, Mighty God, Everlasting Father, Prince of Peace."[29]

The title for Jesus as the Prince of Peace is well known, but this same paragraph gave him two other titles that some may have overlooked, Mighty God and Everlasting Father. So it was clearly written that this descendent of King David was to be none other than God Himself.

What Did Jesus Say About Himself?

"For I have come down from heaven not to do my will but to do the will of him who sent me."[30]

And in another place, "And now, Father, glorify me in your presence with the glory I had with you *before the world began*." (Italics added)[31]

He claimed to be preexistent to his life on earth and to have lived with God the Father before the earth came into existence. He said he came to earth from his eternal dwelling place because his Father wanted him to.

What Did the Followers of Jesus Say About Him?

His disciple John, who wrote one of the four biographies of Jesus, referred to him as the Word. "In the beginning was the Word, and the Word was with God, and the Word was God. ... The Word became flesh and made his dwelling among us. We have seen his glory, the glory of the One and Only, who came from the Father, full of grace and truth."[32]

Some of his followers were slow in believing what he said about himself since his claims were so unusual. It was an enormous shock for his followers when he was crucified. His disciple, Thomas, was so disillusioned by the death of Jesus that we have this record of the conversation when it first was reported to him that Jesus had resurrected:

> Now Thomas (called Didymus), one of the Twelve, was not with the disciples when Jesus came. So the other disciples told him, "We have seen the Lord!"

But he said to them, "Unless I see the nail marks
in his hands and put my finger where the nails
were, and put my hand into his side, I will not
believe it."

A week later his disciples were in the house again,
and Thomas was with them. Though the doors
were locked, Jesus came and stood among them
and said, "Peace be with you!" Then he said to
Thomas, "Put your finger here; see my hands.
Reach out your hand and put it into my side.
Stop doubting and believe."

Thomas said to him, "My Lord and my God!"[33]

If you would like to investigate more about
the resurrection of Jesus, an English lawyer, Frank
Morison, wrote, *Who Moved The Stone?*[34] He was a
rationalist who did not believe in the resurrection
of Jesus. But while he was gathering information
to write a book about the last seven days of Jesus'
life, "to strip it of its overgrowth of primitive beliefs
and dogmatic suppositions ...."[35], to his surprise,
he came to the conclusion that the resurrection of
Jesus was a reality. He had investigated the facts sur-
rounding the resurrection as thoroughly as a lawyer.
He then wrote a different book than what he had
intended, one supporting the resurrection.

I do not present these ideas as proof that Jesus
was God. I present them as evidence that his enemies
understood that he declared himself as such and his
followers believed he was. The Jewish scriptures
of the Old Testament written long before the birth

of Jesus, declared him to be the Messiah and Jesus declared himself the Messiah, the one called, "God with us."

These ideas are important, because in trying to discover who he really was, we need to eliminate the option that he was just a good man. He either must be much more or much less, that is to say, either he is God With Us, or he is a deceiver of the worst type.

In order to convince us of that which would normally be impossible for us to believe, God walking on earth in human form, he would need to leave us with enough evidence to bring us to that conclusion.

From my own perspective, if some person were to so say to me, "I am God," I would consider him to be crazy or self-deceived unless he could offer me proof that he is God. I don't think that the burden of proof lies with me to prove he is not; it would lie with him to prove that he is. Taking this perspective, let's see what we find.

Now, reader, what type of evidence would be necessary for him to convince you he is God? What if he changed an orange into a dove, would that convince you? But the illusionist David Copperfield could do that and we wouldn't know how. That wouldn't convince us that he is God. It seems to me it must be something out of the ordinary, something a man could not do.

This presents a problem. You probably don't believe in miracles. You would probably demand that he present proof he is God by doing something extraordinary. Without realizing it, you have put yourself in a position of denying any evidence that he could use to convince you since you don't believe in miracles. I am asking you, that for the moment, you abandon the position of denying miracles so that you can investigate the subject without prejudice and "a priori" decisions. Let him present his evidences without annulling them ahead of time.

He Demonstrated Control Over the Elements

If there is a creator-God, and if Jesus is he on earth, then he should be able to demonstrate the elements are subject to him, that he is greater than the physical universe and the laws that govern it. The evidences are significant and will be difficult for you to believe if you don't believe God is active on the earth or that Jesus could do these things. If you don't succeed in gaining an open mind, you will reject the following without even considering it. But, away we go!

> Then he got into the boat and his disciples fol-
> lowed him. Without warning, a furious storm
> came up on the lake, so that the waves swept over
> the boat. But Jesus was sleeping. The disciples
> went and woke him, saying, "Lord, save us! We're
> going to drown!"

He replied, "You of little faith, why are you so afraid?" Then he got up and rebuked the winds and the waves, and it was completely calm.

The men were amazed and asked, "What kind of man is this? Even the winds and the waves obey him![36]

The men who accompanied him did not believe he had such power, but they hit the nail on the head when they asked, "What kind of man is this? Even the winds and the waves obey him!" If you had been there, how would you have responded?

He Demonstrated Power Over Life and Death

How can a man demonstrate so much power and authority by just speaking? In the prior example he just spoke to the wind and the waves, nothing more. The same thing happens in the next example.

The next day as they were leaving Bethany, Jesus was hungry. Seeing in the distance a fig tree in leaf, he went to find out if it had any fruit. When he reached it, he found nothing but leaves, because it was not the season for figs. Then he said to the tree, "May no one ever eat fruit from you again." And his disciples heard him say it… In the morning, as they went along, they saw the fig tree withered from the roots. Peter remembered and said to Jesus, "Rabbi, look! The fig tree you cursed has withered!"[37]

I am not going to discuss why he gave this sign to the Jews. We are just interested in observing that Jesus had within him the power of life and death, which he ought to have if he is God.

> Soon afterward, Jesus went to a town called Nain, and his disciples and a large crowd went along with him. As he approached the town gate, a dead person was being carried out—the only son of his mother, and she was a widow. And a large crowd from the town was with her. When the Lord saw her, his heart went out to her and he said, "Don't cry."
>
> Then he went up and touched the coffin, and those carrying it stood still. He said, "Young man, I say to you, get up!" The dead man sat up and began to talk, and Jesus gave him back to his mother.
>
> They were all filled with awe and praised God. "A great prophet has appeared among us," they said. "God has come to help his people."[38]

It was true God had come to help his people. They still didn't understand God was walking among them. What he did, he performed in the most natural way without making a big deal of it. Most of these demonstrations of God-like power, he did in the presence of crowds. And he did the most unsuspecting things. Who would even have dared to ask him to do these things? Just as you are amazed at these things and can scarcely believe they are true, so it was the same with them, "They were all filled with awe."

There are an abundance of examples of his awesome power. The one I would like to focus on next has to do with his power over life and death in the famous example of a man called Lazarus. I appreciate your willingness to stick with me in my presentation of the evidences of the supernatural powers of this man Jesus. As I said previously, before I made my investigations, I too doubted he was any more than a moral teacher, that he was more than a man. I am including more of the background of this event since it is so significant and shows such outstanding power.

> Now a man named Lazarus was sick. He was from Bethany, the village of Mary and her sister Martha. This Mary, whose brother Lazarus now lay sick, was the same one who poured perfume on the Lord and wiped his feet with her hair. So the sisters sent word to Jesus, "Lord, the one you love is sick."[39]

> .....On his arrival, Jesus found that Lazarus had already been in the tomb for four days. Bethany was less than two miles from Jerusalem, and many Jews had come to Martha and Mary to comfort them in the loss of their brother. When Martha heard that Jesus was coming, she went out to meet him, but Mary stayed at home.

> "Lord," Martha said to Jesus, "if you had been here, my brother would not have died. But I

know that even now God will give you whatever you ask." Jesus said to her, "Your brother will rise again."

Martha answered, "I know he will rise again in the resurrection at the last day."

Jesus said to her, "I am the resurrection and the life. He who believes in me will live, even though he dies; and whoever lives and believes in me will never die. Do you believe this?"

"Yes, Lord," she told him, "I believe that you are the Christ, the Son of God, who was to come into the world."

And after she had said this, she went back and called her sister Mary aside. "The Teacher is here," she said, "and is asking for you." When Mary heard this, she got up quickly and went to him. Now Jesus had not yet entered the village, but was still at the place where Martha had met him. When the Jews who had been with Mary in the house, comforting her, noticed how quickly she got up and went out, they followed her, supposing she was going to the tomb to mourn there.

When Mary reached the place where Jesus was and saw him, she fell at his feet and said, "Lord, if you had been here, my brother would not have died."

When Jesus saw her weeping, and the Jews who had come along with her also weeping, he was deeply moved in spirit and troubled. "Where have you laid him?" he asked.

"Come and see, Lord," they replied.

Jesus wept.

Then the Jews said, "See how he loved him!"

But some of them said, "Could not he who opened the eyes of the blind man have kept this man from dying?"

Jesus, once more deeply moved, came to the tomb. It was a cave with a stone laid across the entrance. "Take away the stone," he said.

"But, Lord," said Martha, the sister of the dead man, "by this time there is a bad odor, for he has been there four days."

Then Jesus said, "Did I not tell you that if you believed, you would see the glory of God?"

So they took away the stone. Then Jesus looked up and said, "Father, I thank you that you have heard me. I knew that you always hear me, but I said this for the benefit of the people standing here, that they may believe that you sent me."

When he had said this, Jesus called in a loud voice, "Lazarus, come out!" The dead man came out, his hands and feet wrapped with strips of linen, and a cloth around his face.

Jesus said to them, "Take off the grave clothes and let him go."

Therefore many of the Jews who had come to visit Mary, and had seen what Jesus did, put their faith in him.[40]

He Created

Let's analyze what Jesus did at a wedding feast in Cana, near his hometown of Nazareth.

On the third day a wedding took place at Cana in Galilee. Jesus' mother was there, and Jesus and his disciples had also been invited to the wedding. When the wine was gone, Jesus' mother said to him, "They have no more wine."

"Dear woman, why do you involve me?" Jesus replied. "My time has not yet come."

His mother said to the servants, "Do whatever he tells you."

Nearby stood six stone water jars, the kind used by the Jews for ceremonial washing, each holding from twenty to thirty gallons.

Jesus said to the servants, "Fill the jars with water"; so they filled them to the brim.

Then he told them, "Now draw some out and take it to the master of the banquet."

They did so, and the master of the banquet tasted the water that had been turned into wine. He did not realize where it had come from, though the servants who had drawn the water knew. Then he called the bridegroom aside and said, "Everyone brings out the choice wine first and then the cheaper wine after the guests have had too much to drink; but you have saved the best till now."

This, the first of his miraculous signs, Jesus performed at Cana in Galilee. He thus revealed his glory, and his disciples put their faith in him.[41]

As we consider what happened, it is important to note the quantity of water that was transformed, six containers of 20 to 30 gallons each, between 120 and 150 gallons. This wasn't a little "hocus pocus" said over a glass with a handkerchief over it. No wonder his disciples "put their faith in him."

Now, in the 21st century, we know water is composed of hydrogen and oxygen. Wine contains an enormous amount of minerals besides these two elements. How could he change water into wine without doing an act of creation? If the event is true, it is significant evidence Jesus was not just a good man with good ideas. He was the Creator who had come to earth to walk among us.

He Could Read Their Minds

On many occasions Jesus must have scared people out of their wits. Imagine if you met a man who could read your mind and answer your mental, unvoiced thoughts! It would be scary. That's what Jesus did on a number of occasions.

> Since they could not get him to Jesus because of the crowd, they made an opening in the roof above Jesus and, after digging through it, lowered the mat the paralyzed man was lying on. When Jesus saw their faith, he said to the paralytic, "Son, your sins are forgiven."
>
> Now some teachers of the law were sitting there, thinking to themselves, "Why does this fellow talk like that? He's blaspheming! Who can forgive sins but God alone?"
>
> Immediately Jesus knew in his spirit that this was what they were thinking in their hearts, and he said to them, "Why are you thinking these things? Which is easier: to say to the paralytic, 'Your sins are forgiven,' or to say, 'Get up, take your mat and walk'? But that you may know that the Son of Man has authority on earth to forgive sins…" He said to the paralytic, "I tell you, get up, take your mat and go home" He got up, took his mat and walked out in full view of them all. This amazed everyone and they praised God, saying, "We have never seen anything like this!"[42]

To sum it up:

The life of Jesus is marked again and again with evidences he was more than a man. I hope by now you are thinking that Jesus was much more than you thought up to this point. I hope you doubt he was only a man. If so, could he still be alive? Let's now consider that.

Is It Possible That Jesus Still Lives?

Life After Death

Following the idea that Jesus could be God in human form, we need to leave the idea of the historic Jesus and consider the Jesus of the present. If it is true that Jesus died 2,000 years ago and that, after three days he rose from the dead, then he ought to be alive somewhere. The claim is that he not only raised others from the dead but that he himself resurrected. Speaking about his own life Jesus said, "No one takes it from me, but I lay it down of my own accord. I have authority to lay it down and authority to take it up again."[43]

This is the main reason his disciples continued after his death to follow him, and a major reason why his present followers follow him. To follow him if he is dead doesn't make much sense. He promised eternal life to his followers, but if he isn't alive, why should we believe we would have a life after death? He also promised to help his followers daily, which he wouldn't be able to do if he were dead.

Why did the apostles follow him after his death? The answer is simple, because they saw him a number of times after his death. He appeared to them telling them that he is the Lord of the Universe, "Then Jesus came to them and said, 'All authority in heaven and on earth has been given to me. Therefore go and make disciples of all nations ...'"[44]

The last time they saw him on earth this is what they claimed happened, "After he said this, he was taken up before their very eyes, and a cloud hid him from their sight."[45]

The apostle Paul in his defense of the resurrection talks about eye witnesses, "...and that He was buried, and that He was raised on the third day according to the Scriptures, and that He appeared to Cephas, then to the twelve. After that He appeared to more than five hundred brethren at one time, most of whom remain until now, but some have fallen asleep; then He appeared to James, then to all the apostles; and last of all, as it were to one untimely born, He appeared to me also."[46]

There are a great number of religious "Christians" who have no contact with the resurrected Jesus. They only have religion. Another great number of people have encountered Jesus and live in the reality of him, his promises, and his power.

This will probably create confusion for you, but it is confusion you will need to resolve. I have no doubt you will be able to, for you already have probably suspected there are real Christians as well as pseudo ones. You will be able to identify the difference between those who only profess to know Jesus and those who demonstrate by their lives that they do.

You can see the difference in the real ones by the presence of the transforming power of Jesus. If you don't see the transforming power in the life of a person who declares himself or herself a Christian, then you ought to doubt the truth of his or her declaration. I considered myself a real Christian when I was not. I was just religious and was not aware of the difference. I came to realize my error when I encountered the living Jesus and began to experience his transforming power.

You may ask in what way does he show that he is alive? How do you recognize his power? One way is how those who really know him live. Four ways stand out to me: their love for others, their interior peace in a variety of circumstances, their understanding of the meaning of life, and the fact that God responds to their requests.

The Evidence of Love

The love God develops in his people is not a love that is self-centered. It is a love from above and isn't interested in personal profit. It only looks to benefit the other person without personal gain. Probably you don't even believe this type of love exists. However, if you encounter a true follower of Jesus you will discover its existence. This is what took me by surprise when I came to know the living Jesus. Without even asking for it this kind of love entered my life. It was evidence that I had been put into contact with God. This contact with God did not come with great emotion; it was more like a whole new viewpoint of life. I began to seek the good of others without any thought of what I would get out of it.

This love exists in me in spite of the fact I am a very imperfect person. I do have my self-centeredness, but it doesn't annul the love from God that lives within me. This love entered me with such force, that after graduating from college and spending a year in business, I left the job and spent full time helping others encounter this love. I didn't do it for a better salary, for some kind of fame, or even so that I could feel good about myself. My only motive was this driving love that possessed my life, this love given by the risen Christ. With this I don't mean to imply that everyone who experiences this love ought to quit his or her job. Each person will do what this love guides them to do. Some will feel that they should stay exactly where they are so that the people whom they work with and relate to will be able to experience and observe this love in their midst.

The love operating in Mother Teresa of Calcutta made her famous. It was the love of the living Jesus manifesting itself in her. However, this love is not for a privileged few. It is for you and me and for all that will draw near to Jesus with a sincere heart. It is the mark of the true followers of Jesus. As he said: "By this all men will know that you are my disciples, if you love one another."[47]

The Evidence of Peace of Heart

The experience of inner peace is one of the most common and immediate characteristics people usually experience when God enters their lives. You may not even be aware you lack it. We are so accustomed to comparing ourselves with those in our surroundings that if others around us lack something we often are not aware that we lack it also.

When I was young my parents sent me every summer to my great uncle's ranch. I helped to bring in the harvest of the ranches that surrounded us. We were paid by the piece, that is, we got paid according to the amount we harvested. Those who worked fast and hard earned more than those who were slower. Everyone worked hard even in the heat of the day. This was the only work that I knew.

When I was about nineteen I discovered to my surprise that the people in the city earned more than I did, worked under easier conditions, stopped for coffee, sat in comfortable chairs, etc. Because on the ranch everyone worked hard under the hot sun, I thought that was what everyone experienced.

Peace is like that. If you live without it, it is like working in the hot sun and not being aware that there is another option. The day Jesus entered my life, a peace that I had never known before also entered my life. As the love that entered my life was totally unexpected, so the peace also was a total surprise. Why hadn't people told me beforehand about this amazing spiritual treasure? Possibly they had, but maybe what they had to say didn't hold any value for me at the time.

One of my friends, who is a doctor, arrived at faith in Jesus as a student of medicine. When I met him he didn't have this faith. Some years after, my friend told me, "Jack, I very much appreciated all of the arguments and evidences you presented to me about the existence of God. But those things were not what convinced me. As I visited your home and was with your family, I sensed peace. I kept returning to your home hoping I could find the peace that was evident there, until I finally found it."

While living in California for a while, my wife and I made friends with a Mexican couple. We studied the life of Jesus together since our friends were searching for answers to life and searching for God. It wasn't long before the wife, and later her husband, came to the conclusion that Jesus is alive and desired to enter her life. One afternoon she prayed and asked Jesus to come into her heart and to live with her.

Two weeks later we all got together and I noticed she was very upset. It isn't normal for someone who just met Christ to be so upset. I asked what the problem was. She told us she was living with psychological scars and a profound nervous disorder. One cause was the trauma of experiencing a deadly earthquake in Mexico City. She had also developed extreme fears. She couldn't even shower or wash her hair without her husband nearby for fear that someone would enter the house uninvited and grab her. As a result, she was seeing a psychologist.

I guided her to a promise of God that was for those trusting in Him, a promise about peace.

"Do not be anxious about anything, but in everything, by prayer and petition, with thanksgiving, present your requests to God. And the peace of God, which transcends all understanding, will guard your hearts and your minds in Christ Jesus."[48]

She returned home trusting in this promise. As Joann and I drove home in the car I commented to her that a person with a mental problem so significant could suffer under it for years before she found a solution. I doubted that God would change her quickly.

The next week, you wouldn't guess what happened. We had an earthquake with the epicenter being in the very the town where she lived! I thought, "Poor woman, now she will really be in trouble!" Two weeks passed before we saw her again. She was filled with peace! She told me the same night we gave her that promise, she experienced an unusual calmness of spirit. She immediately lost the fear of washing her hair while she was alone at home. When the earthquake hit she didn't get excited at all. She lives today with the quiet peace of spirit that Jesus gave her that evening when she heard the promise, "And the peace of God, which transcends all understanding", and it became hers.

This leads us to consider the promises of Jesus and his power to respond to our requests. The night prior to his death, knowing that he was going to die, he said to those who trusted in him: "Until now you have not asked for anything in my name. Ask and you will receive, and your joy will be complete."[49]

Wouldn't his followers abandon their trust in Jesus within a couple of months after his death if they discovered his teaching was a lie? If they asked in his name according to his promise and they only experienced a profound silence from deep space, wouldn't they become bitter people as a result of the deception that they would have experienced? This didn't happen because they were not deceived! He filled their lives with the joy he promised. They experienced his continual response to their requests from his new place outside of planet earth. All of those who receive him and follow him, to this day, experience the joy of this promise of the living Jesus.

The Evidence of the Living Jesus' Power to Answer Requests

The answers to requests made in the name of Jesus are one of the things followers of Jesus have in common. It is also one of the easiest things to confirm. All you have to do is draw near to one who truly knows him and observe how Jesus continually responds to him or her. If a scientist wants to know the properties of a substance, he needs to test it. If you, with sincerity, would like to know if Jesus is alive today, find a true follower of his. Ask him or her about their prayers to him. Observe firsthand how these requests are answered. If this person is an authentic believer you will normally find them quite safe to be around and you won't need to be afraid of being with him or her. They are quite harmless. Besides they would be happy to show you what Jesus is doing for them.

I think that answered prayer is one of the most significant evidences of the existence of God and of the truth of Jesus. I continue to be profoundly impressed that Jesus listens to me and answers me. When people ask me for evidences of the existence of God, I usually mention the fact that God continually answers me.

One who has not yet found God may have difficulty believing that he responds and that the results or circumstances come from his intervention. In part, it is because the answer is often as personal as the request. One can give you innumerable examples of these answers, but you could deny they are truly from God. If I ask Jesus for something and he gives me the answer needed, you could always say that it happened by chance.

But it happens too often to be chance. Let me give you an example. If I were raised in the jungle and didn't know about electricity and I entered a room and flipped on the light switch and the lights went on, I would be surprised and doubting that my action had turned on the lights. But if each time I flicked the switch on, the lights went on, I would draw the conclusion that there was a relationship between touching the switch and the lights going on. Prayer is like that. If an answer comes just once, I might say it was just by chance. But if I pray often and find answers often, I must come to the conclusion that there is a relationship between the prayer and the answer. There is someone upstairs listening and responding. In this case it is Jesus, the living one.

I decided early on in my relationship with God that I would give more importance to the formation of my spirit and eternal values than to the temporal or material. While in college, I needed to work during the summers to finance my college education. One summer there was a two week seminar offered by a Christian organization for spiritual development. It was offered right in the middle of the summer. No business would employ me for the summer if I were going to take two weeks off in the middle of the job. There were a lot of college students looking for work who would work the full summer, and few jobs available in my city. But following my pattern of giving priority to my spiritual development, I decided to trust God to help me out.

A friend told me of a business that was going to start hiring for the summer so I went for an interview. The department head offered me the job but I told him that I couldn't accept the job unless he would guarantee to let me attend this Christian conference in the middle of the summer. He gave me a strange look. I knew there were a dozen other candidates lined up for the job who would attach no such condition.

I remember clearly how he turned around to a calendar hanging behind him where he had marked in the vacation dates of his regular employees. He discovered the exact dates I needed free were the only ones that he had no one going on vacation. It was actually a help to him not to have to pay me for those dates. He hired me. I believe God had answered my request for work and for growth in my relationship with him. It would be hard to call this chance.

My wife and I and our first two children were living in England when some very serious incidents occurred. My wife and I had gone on a business trip leaving a young woman in our home with our children to care for them. Our younger child, our daughter, was two years old at the time.

In the children's bedroom there were bunk beds. One day, while cleaning the room, the young lady sat the two-year-old on the upper bunk although it was off bounds to our little one. She fell off of the bunk and injured her leg. The woman took the child to the doctor and the doctor said she was O.K. When we got home one week after the fall, we discovered our daughter was unable to walk and was in great pain. Another visit to the doctor confirmed she had a fractured leg.

She wore a cast for a while, but when it was taken off she was unable to walk and could only crawl. This carried on for about three months and left us greatly concerned for her. I assume that the pain of trying to walk on that fractured leg for a week had made her afraid to walk on the leg at all. We couldn't make our two-year-old understand that she could walk without pain.

During this same time another complication arose in the family. My wife had developed a painful ingrown toenail. (Forgive the personal, disagreeable details.) Our four-year-old son would be playing around not paying attention, as four-year-olds do, and was constantly stepping on his mother's toe. Ouch! The result was that whenever he would go near her, she would push him away so that he wouldn't step on her. He began to get the impression that his mother was rejecting him. Bad deal!

I was very concerned for both situations. Since I am in touch with God, I was asking him for solutions but none came. God doesn't give us everything we ask just because we ask. He may put conditions on receiving and may sometimes have other plans that are difficult for us to understand or accept.

After getting no response from God, I went upstairs to talk alone with him. I told him I had been praying for three months about my daughter, and she still wasn't walking. Instead of accusing God, I began considering my own life. I realized that I was asking without faith, which God said was the element necessary for him to answer. After some minutes of reflection I came to the point of believing he would answer. I left this time of prayer with the confidence that God would grant my request. However, I didn't confide this to anyone at the time.

When we all got up the next morning my two-year-old got out of bed and started running around the house as if nothing had happened! From that day on, the four-year-old never again stepped on his mother's foot. It was as if God had put an invisible barrier protecting her foot!

These personal family incidents carry no importance to you, but they were tremendously important to our family. From these two examples, the first of getting time off from work for my spiritual development, and the second of solving a physical, mundane, problem for the family, you get a picture of God helping us no matter what the problem. These are two examples chosen from among the many, almost daily, responses God gives our family. We experience him constantly in observable, concrete ways.

It isn't unusual for people, when in desperation, to prove the power of Jesus, as is exemplified in the Gospels.

When this man heard that Jesus had arrived in
Galilee from Judea, he went to him and begged
him to come and heal his son, who was close
to death.

"Unless you people see miraculous signs and
wonders," Jesus told him, "you will never
believe."

The royal official said, "Sir, come down before
my child dies." Jesus replied, "You may go. Your
son will live."

The man took Jesus at his word and departed.
While he was still on the way, his servants met
him with the news that his boy was living. When
he inquired as to the time when his son got better,
they said to him, "The fever left him yesterday
at the seventh hour."

Then the father realized that this was the exact time at which Jesus had said to him, "Your
son will live." So he and all his household believed.[50]

I hope these illustrations of the power of Jesus,
who is alive today, will cause you to think about how
he would be able to change your life if you could
come to trust in him.

And now we will consider that very question.
"What would my life be like if Jesus were a part of
it?"

Chapter 8

· ·

What Would a New Life With God Be Like?

L et's suppose for a minute someone reading this book has come to believe in Jesus, and has invited him into his life to accompany him in everything he does. What would his life be like? What could he expect? How would God treat him?

He Would Discover That God Has the Heart of a Father

God would treat you like a father would treat his newborn child. Are you a father or a mother? Do you remember the day your first child was born? What kind of emotions did you experience? Did you frown and say to yourself, "I wonder if he will behave?" Of course not, you were filled with joy and some awe at the child that was now yours. Your very own first child! How amazing! You weren't thinking about what the child ought to do, you were thinking about what you would need to do for your newborn. The first thing you probably did was to take the child in your arms, stroke him or her, and look closely to observe every little detail. That is similar to God's attitude toward you if you have just become his child.

When you come into this new world as a new-born, the initial thing the Father does is to wash you. We wash physical babies with physical water. God washes his babies spiritually, that is, he cleanses them from all the sins of their lives up to that point. He makes their spirit clean and gives them full pardon. To find out what God thinks, let's listen to what he says: "He saved us, not because of righteous things we had done, but because of his mercy. He saved us through the washing of rebirth and renewal by the Holy Spirit."[51]

"If we confess our sins, he is faithful and just and will forgive us our sins and purify us from all unrighteousness."[52]

You will have a sense of cleanness that will be new. Have you made some bad mistakes in your life? The bad things we have done in life, things we would like to forget, are like dirty and worn out clothes. When God forgives you, it is as though he takes away your dirty, old clothes and freely gives you new clothes fitting for your new position as a son or daughter of the Eternal Father. It is almost too much to believe, but God loves doing wonderful things for us. He teaches us that in his sight, faith in Jesus counts for everything we need. It counts for cleanness, good works, and acceptance to God. He gives us the good works as a gift that we could never have come up with.

There are people who are constantly looking for forgiveness. It is as if they are continually washing dirty hands without being able to get them clean. The dirt is stuck on. How sad when someone feels his soul is dirty and can't find any way to clean it. Part of the Good News, that is, the Gospel, is that God has found a cleanser that does the job, one that eliminates all stains without leaving a trace.

"'Come now, let us reason together,' says the Lord. 'Though your sins are like scarlet, they shall be as white as snow; though they are red as crimson, they shall be like wool.'"[53]

He gives you a full pardon, without reservation. You can rest from any continual attempts to cleanse yourself. It's over if Jesus has entered your life. In God's eyes your interior is clean. But I want to warn you many people may not forgive you. Humanity is not as forgiving as God. In spite of this, you can live in peace with yourself knowing you really are clean inside.

He Would Discover That God Enjoys His Companionship

God has an enormous desire to be with you. Upon receiving Jesus into your life, the Holy Spirit of God comes in to live with you.[54] You will never be alone again. God has come into your life to enjoy you forever. He will accompany you wherever you go. In this companionship he will talk with you.

You may ask how he will speak to you. Will he speak in an audible voice? How will he do this? It is a very natural question.

Recently I was golfing and conversing with one of my foursome. My companion discovered I sleep very little and that I had risen at 4:00 a.m. He asked me what I do when I get up so early. I decided to be frank with him and told him I read the paper and also talk with God. I listen to him as I read the Bible.

As my friend is a skeptic, he asked scornfully, "And does he answer you?"

I answered, "Yes, but not in an audible voice, but in some way in the quietness of my spirit, or by a part of the Bible I am reading." God is alive and present and desires to communicate with me.

Since I know this is all new to you, let me describe it for you from my own experience. After finishing college I was employed by a printing firm in San Francisco. One day I went to an engineering firm to try to sell them on our printing since we specialized in technical work. To get the account I lied about the equipment we had. I knew beforehand God never lies to us and he doesn't want us to lie to others.

As I was returning to the office my mind was flooded with thoughts from God on how much he loved me. I knew that these thoughts came directly from him. I realized at that time God could have filled my mind with thoughts of reproof for the deed I had done. But instead of that he chose another way to deal with me. Reminding me of the enormous love that he has for me was very effective in bringing me to the decision to stop lying.

The Spirit of God will speak to your inner person and you will recognize his voice when he does.

You will discover the Bible is a sure way to hear the voice of God. He reveals himself through the Bible. When Jesus enters your life he will make the Scriptures alive and they will become a source of the voice of God for you. Try to read it every day, not as an obligation or a religious act, but simply with the desire to communicate with God. I count it a privilege to listen to his ideas, his voice, and to get acquainted with him.

If you haven't yet come to the point of opening your heart to him, you will be questioning inside yourself what listening to God is all about. How can this be? Well, it may be outside of your experience, but not outside of mine. Try not to think of this as unreal or a mistake, just because you haven't experienced it. There are a lot of things in life that you haven't experienced yet.

It is possible to verify that God exists. Even if you haven't arrived at a position of trust in Jesus where you could let him into your life, you may have come to suspect that he exists. If you are ready to take a risk, there does remain a step you can take in verifying all of this. God speaks through the

Bible to those who trust him, but he also desires to communicate with those who doubt his existence. You can speak directly to God telling him that you are not sure of his existence, but that if he does exist you would like to know him.

After a simple and sincere conversation like this with God, begin to read the Gospel of John in the New Testament. Expect him to respond to your desire to know him and to begin to reveal things about himself to you from these readings. Don't be in a rush, he might not speak immediately. Just keep reading.

He Would Discover that God Enjoys Listening to Him

For those of us who have received Jesus, we not only have the privilege of listening to God, but also the assurance that God listens to us. Jesus said to his disciples: "Until now you have not asked for anything in my name. Ask and you will receive, and your joy will be complete."[55]

When I had religion without knowing God, I can't recall any time when God answered a request I made to him. When I finally came to know him I was not aware of the above promise. It took me a while to realize God was very interested in my speaking to him. He wanted to answer any request I made that was a good one. By that I mean, he doesn't want to help me do bad things, things that harm others.

Now I speak to him often. He answers my requests for both significant and insignificant things. He is very interested in my whole life. Others have written entire books about how he answers us.[56] If you want to know more about God answering, a good place to start is by reading the four accounts of the life of Jesus, the first four books of the New Testament. As you read, watch for personal requests people made of Jesus. There are plenty of examples. The Jesus who lived then is the same Jesus who lives and answers now.

He Gives Us a New Orientation to Life and New Purpose

He leads us into purposes that are worthy of eternity. The average person finds his purposes fall into two categories. One is the pursuit of material well-being for himself and his family. The other is working for the well-being of this present material society.

Up until now the focus of your life has been the short dimension, the life of 70 to 90 years. But this is only the beginning of a much longer life, one that goes on forever. God is eternal and has granted you a life that is eternal. Death is only a change in our life and the entrance into an existence without physical limitations. Right now I live in two dimensions. One consists of my physical body that is so temporary. The other is the spirit that dwells within my body, the part of me that lasts forever.

Before coming to know Christ my constant con-
cerns were to make a lot of money, to have a good
time, to have a good job, and to find a woman with
whom I could share my life.

These are important things, but only for this
present life. When God enters your life he broadens
your perspective to include the eternal. You begin
to want to know him, the Eternal. You find you also
become interested in others around you coming
to know him and adding the eternal dimension to
their lives. Before you lived primarily for your own
benefit, now you naturally seek to benefit others.
Before you were the center of your universe, now
both God and others become significant. This is
called loving God and loving others. Somehow you
discover that self is peripheral compared to the other
two. Joy does not enter your life by self-fulfillment;
it enters by seeking the good of others. That is the
nature of this new life in God.

You discover that while you are seeking the good
of others, God is taking care of your welfare. It's not
that you are left hanging without anything, it is just
the opposite. You are left in the center of God with
everything. "He who did not spare his own Son, but
gave him up for us all–how will he not also, along
with him, graciously give us all things?"[57]

Ever since I stopped making self-interest my
primary pursuit and began pursuing the benefit of
others, I have entered into a life full of meaning.
Nothing gives me more pleasure than to see another
person encounter God. While I am seeking the

benefit of others, God takes pleasure in seeking my benefit and providing everything I need, a multitude of good things.

I don't want to give the impression that my life is plush and without difficulties. It isn't, but God meets the most profound desires of my heart. Everyone searches for peace. I already have it. Everyone wishes to be loved. I am loved beyond comprehension. Everyone wants to be appreciated. God abounds in his appreciation of me and also fills my life with the appreciation of many other people, including my wife and children.

The central idea of this new life is to walk with Jesus, the Ruler of the Universe. He promised to constantly accompany those who know him. To walk with him also means to live as he lived. It is not possible to walk with him and to live contrary to the way he lived. Study his life and you will be able to understand how he lived. The Gospels demonstrate how he thought and lived. Read them regularly to grow in your comprehension of what his life was like. Then live that way.

Some people think receiving Jesus by faith means to live a life full of religious activities and rituals. This couldn't be farther from the truth. Rather than doing religious things, this life is about living as he lived, but in your own context of life. The day I received Jesus I almost decided not to, because I thought I would have to live a "religious" life! The thought of that scared me to death since I neither wanted to nor knew how. But as I thought about it

I realized that wasn't necessary. Jesus only invited me to live in the way he lived, compassionate, caring, full of love for and trust in God, not being "religious."

Here is how I encountered this new life.

I was the youngest of three children and was born in California. I guess most people consider their family "normal" and I was no exception. My dad was a factory worker who later became a personnel director. They now call this the people resource department. My mother was a teacher. We attended a church but my dad usually slept through the sermons and eventually he stopped joining us.

By the time I hit my teens the family was disintegrating. My father had become an alcoholic and conflict at home became the menu of the day until he finally left home. A divorce was in the works later on down the road.

As a family we had spent a lot of time fishing and hiking in the Sierra Nevada. I learned to love the great outdoors and so began my college career majoring in Forestry. In biology and geology classes evolution became a major issue for my consideration. This was a shock, conflicting with my childhood training which had been religious and had embraced the idea of a Creator. I entered my first true conflict of values and life orientation.

The conflict involved more than simply the question of a Creator or evolution. My entire religious upbringing came under scrutiny. I discovered I had no firm foundation for anything I believed. I asked myself why I believed in Christianity, and the answer came: "Because I was raised to believe it." I discovered this belief was the belief of my teachers and parents, but not my own.

So I began a sincere search for the truth of the matter. I put up for question both evolution and creation. If there is a God, which religion expresses him? Though I was raised in a Christian environment, I became willing to become a Muslim if that is where my search for the truth led. I read works by atheists such as Marx and Lenin. I considered three religious books, the Koran, the Bible and the Book of Mormon among other writings.

For various reasons, some mentioned earlier in this book, I found the Bible to be the book that convinced me that God exists and that Jesus is the Son of God. As I read the Gospels, the accounts of the life of Jesus, I found them so powerful that I became convinced that he is the Son of God as he said he is.

So, it seems I had arrived at the end of the road. My search had begun with doubting all my early beliefs, and now I had resolved these doubts to my satisfaction. Was this the end of the road? No. For the journey to end there would have been something like a man who smells a bakery and follows the scent to the front door but stops there, never entering to taste what is offered, saying, "I have found it." I had tasted nothing, only satisfied my mind with answers. The tasting was yet to come.

I made it a habit to read the New Testament. One day as I was finishing reading, I saw a statement that struck me like a blow: "And this is the testimony: God has given us eternal life, and this life is in his Son. He who has the Son has life; he who does not have the Son of God does not have life."[58]

I was struck that since I had come to believe the Bible, I assumed I was a Christian and would gain eternal life. However, this statement says, "he who does not have the Son of God does not have life."

I thought, "I believe in Jesus but I don't have him. I only believe about him. How would someone have, or possess him?" I had no idea. The end of my search had left me outside of the bakery. What a disappointment!

I did continue reading and a few days later and a few pages farther on I came upon the answer to how I (and anyone) could "have" the Son of God, Jesus. I read that Jesus said, "Here I am! I stand at the door and knock. If anyone hears my voice and opens the door, I will come in and eat with him, and he with me."[59] Rather than my standing outside of the bakery looking in, Jesus was standing outside of the door to my life asking if he could enter!

I still had some questions I needed to resolve, but after a few days I invited him into my life just as I would someone who was knocking at the door of my home. Speaking out loud, I invited Jesus to bring me eternal life and to help me live. I promised to follow him on the condition that he would give me the strength to do it. After making this invitation to him and being assured that he had responded, I went to bed with peace and slept. I had the confidence that he came in because I had come to the conclusion that he is God. If God makes a promise he fulfills it. He had said, "You open the door, and I will come in!"

About three months later I looked at my life and discovered, much to my surprise, that I was being transformed. I now loved people without even trying to. I was helping them and thinking about them just naturally. How amazing! This transformation continues to this day along with many other changes.

But what would make God want to enter our lives and enjoy "dining" with us?

Chapter 9

Could God Really Be Interested In You?

What Does God Think of You?

Someone may ask you, "What do you think of God?" The answer is interesting and important. But the question that is far more important is what does God think of you?

You may be one of those who think God is not even aware of your existence. You may be thinking if there is an eternal God, enormous, ruling over the entire universe, he won't even be aware of your existence. You are one person among billions! Besides, how could man be significant when there is so much space, so many planets, stars and galaxies? You may be thinking he doesn't even know you exist. Until now you haven't seen any indication that he is aware of you.

Or perhaps you are among the group who would be totally frightened if you thought God was aware of you. In your mind he is the implacable Judge of the universe who sees everything everywhere. You see him as a being that you would want to avoid at all costs. Do you imagine him as crouched waiting for the smallest mistake so that he can lunge at you and punish you? Or perhaps you think he even perversely would make you punish yourself. Maybe his delight is in making people suffer. If that were the case it would be natural for you to exclaim, "I hope God never thinks about me!"

Yes, God does think about you, but not with this attitude.

The God I have come to know is everywhere. He has seen us from the beginning of our conception and during our formation in the womb. What could alarm you is that he has observed everything you have done from the time you left your mother's womb to the very moment of your reading this sentence. If you see him only as a Judge, you will want to avoid him. But I have come to understand he is also a Father and responds as a father. As a father he would have delighted in your first steps, he would have viewed your first fall with compassion. He participated in the first joy of your heart, and in your first heartbreak.

He has followed closely the formation of your personality and of your thought life. He knows perfectly how you have come to be what you are and to think as you do. He knows you feel lost, doubting your life has a purpose, not knowing why you exist or what the future holds and what life will become. He knows life is a mystery for you. That your life may only consist of an attempt to fill it with meaning, significance, and pleasure. That all of your attempts to find significance and meaning to life have been futile. He isn't coldly evaluating you as if you were some curious object. He does know you inside and out and understands the entire process of how you came to be what you are.

What does he think about you? Whatever it is, he is under no illusion. He knows the truth, the whole truth about you. Knowing it all, how would he think about you? Would he love you, hate you, or perhaps find you tasteless, insipid, only wanting to ignore you?

I am enormously grateful God has revealed how he thinks about us. If it depended on our capacity to deduce or speculate, we would not know anything for sure. The Bible is known as The Word of God. In the life of Jesus Christ, God's thoughts toward us are revealed. He has both said and shown in action that we have enormous value in his eyes. He declares that he would like us to live with him to experience the depths of his love for us continually, both in this life and in our eternal existence after death.

God's Search For Those Who Are Distanced From Him

What does God say about his search for you? He is saying, "I want you to be with me. You have retreated from me and I am working on how I can convince you to desire to know me." This is basically what he means when he says in the Bible, "For God has not chosen to pour out his anger upon us but to save us through our Lord Jesus Christ; he died for us *so that we can live with him forever* (italics mine), whether we are dead or alive at the time of his return."[60]

Does it seem strange to you that God would want your friendship and companionship? He is a being who deeply desires to be with you. His expressed desire is to enjoy your presence both now and for eternity. What a marvelous thing! He thinks about you! I'll bet you never thought God was like this. The primary idea of the Sacred Scriptures, the Bible, is there is a God who is seeking to reconcile people who have distanced themselves from him. Some people are not only distanced, but they also hate him and consider him their enemy. It is the age-old story of a love lost, of a Being who will not rest in his search to reclaim his beloved, you and me, and all humanity.

As you read the life of Jesus in the Gospels, you will see this theme repeated over and over again in parables and human encounters with Jesus. Possibly you have thought that your sins, or shortcomings, are a barrier between you and God. That is not the case! Yes they are the cause of the separation, but there is a solution to the cause. The main barrier to your not knowing and enjoying God is your desire to keep distance between you and him.

If you have read the Gospels, especially Luke's Gospel, do you remember a man named Zacchaeus? He was vertically challenged and climbed a tree to be able to see over the crowds and catch a glimpse of Jesus as he passed by.[61] He was a wealthy man, a tax collector for the Romans who occupied Palestine at that time. In the eyes of the Jews he was a traitor, a collaborator of the occupying army that governed them. Besides collaborating with the enemy, tax collectors were infamous for their corruption. They used their position to unjustly enrich themselves (not a totally new story). People hated them. They were marginalized from society. They were not allowed in church. They could not worship God with others.

How greatly annoyed the crowd must have been when Jesus saw Zacchaeus sitting on a tree limb watching him and asked to go to his house to have dinner! Jesus showed no concern over the disapproval of the crowd for he was intent on recovering a person lost to him and God. This was his mission in life. Jesus took the initiative to reconcile people to God. Zacchaeus responded with excitement to the loving initiative on God's part and was reconciled that very evening. Read it yourself!

The message from God was, "You aren't religious, you have cheated people out of what was rightfully theirs, people despise you, at times you despise yourself. That's O.K., I love you with an extraordinary love. I am searching for you. Please don't run from me, I won't hurt you."

That evening as Zacchaeus expressed his delight at God's acceptance of him, Jesus informed the on-lookers, who resented his acceptance of Zacchaeus, "Today salvation has come to this house, because this man, too, is a son of Abraham. For the Son of Man came to seek and to save what was lost."[62]

On another occasion Jesus encountered a woman who was despised by others.[63] But more than being despised, she must have been disillusioned with life, confused and disorientated.

At that time, the country towns of Palestine were small villages. This woman's situation was known to everyone. According to the customs of the times, a father or other relative arranged the marriage. Her father had sought a husband for his daughter. After a period of time her husband rejected and divorced her. She probably returned to her father's house. Later she married again and was rejected and divorced the second time. What a disaster for her in a small town! But wait, that is not all. This happened five times! Finally, she went to live with a man without marrying him. Could she not stand another divorce? Did life have too much disaster for her?

Jesus encountered her at the city well drawing water alone, at a time of the day when the other women of the village would not be there. She was shunned. But he reached out to her. He offered her eternal life with God. As she conversed with him, she declared that she was confused about which was the "right" religion and she looked to Jesus for some guidance and clarification. He said, "…. true worshipers will worship the Father in spirit and truth, for they are the kind of worshipers the Father seeks."[64]

Jesus had come to earth on behalf of the Father to look for people who were distanced from him. But it is not just people in difficult circumstances who are distanced from God. Jesus came to search out people who are admired and respected by society. Are you in the respected category? God is searching for you the same as for the despised ones. There is no reason that you cannot experience the love God has for you no matter which category you are in. Jesus was calling anyone and everyone to become reconciled to God. A just and upright man, a religious man, Nicodemus, came to be reconciled to God.[65] There was a wealthy young man, living a comfortable life, who was interested in gaining an assurance of eternal life. But he wasn't able to accept the ideas of Jesus. They were too difficult for him to accept and he walked away. As he was going Jesus watched him, loving him even as he distanced himself, for Jesus had invited him to join his other disciples.[66]

Steps Toward An Encounter With God

Jesus went around teaching that God was searching to draw people to himself no matter what category they fit into. It didn't matter if they were moral
or amoral, respected or not respected. Everyone was
welcome. Each person was invited, not forced. He
invites, you make the decision. He is inviting you,
reader, to decide whether you want to be reconciled
to him or whether you want to tell him to get lost.
God has made clear his desire to be with you. What
will you do with his invitation?

God has made it clear he wants your friendship,
for the two of you to walk together down life's road.
Can we steal, hate, deceive, hurt others, and at the
same time walk with God? Can we treat God as if
he didn't exist and still walk with him? Is it possible
to reject God's values and principles and yet to walk
with him? Can two people who walk two different
roads walk together?

The first step in walking with God is to come to
agreement with him. It is to admit inside of ourselves
that our way of living has been mistaken and his
way of living is the right one. All of the ways that
honor God and are beneficial to man usually are his
ways. It is like two people on a path who see each
other from a distance. As they draw near and talk
together about the direction they are going, one of
them draws the conclusion that he has been going
in the wrong direction and turns to join the other,
going in his direction. We need to understand God's
way is to help others, to live out justice and mercy,

to be beneficial to humanity. Our way has not been this way. The decision to leave our present and past way of living for a better one, God's way, is the first step to walking with him.

The second step has to do with trust. If we choose a new, unknown road will we follow someone down that new road if we don't believe he knows where he is going? If someone is lost in a forest, will they follow someone they don't trust? Jesus said, "I am the light of the world. Whoever follows me will never walk in darkness, but will have the light of life."[67] I want to encourage you to read his biography. I believe what he says and does will convince you that he really is the Son of God, and that the above quote is true. It will be impossible to follow him unless you do draw the conclusion that he is the Son of God, and that you can trust him.

If you come to agree with Jesus about his way of living and believe he is the Son of God and worthy of following, only one step remains to be taken. That is the decision to follow him. To come to believe his path is the right path but to not follow in this path is to reject it. The decision needs to be, "I will walk with you and I will leave my old path of living."

Some years ago I found myself at this crossroad. After some months of investigation and discovery, I arrived at the conclusion that my way of living was mistaken and Jesus is the Son of God. But I stopped right there. I hesitated to make the decision to actually follow him.

I was afraid to make this commitment. Where would his paths lead me since they were so different from mine? I knew that I lacked the will power to change myself. I knew I couldn't live his way, it was beyond me. How sad, I had found the way of life, eternal life, and I couldn't follow it!

I had two fears. The first was that I would not be able to follow in his paths. Second, I was afraid of what he would do with my life if he were to control it. This second fear was overcome as I read the Gospels, the biographies of the life of Jesus. His love came through so strong I realized there was nothing to fear from him. I realized if I were to follow him he would not destroy my life; he would fulfill it and make it a success because of his love for me.

The only obstacle that remained was the realization that I would not be able to live up to his high way of life. As I read his life I came to understand that he was offering the power and ability to follow him. I did not need to find this power within myself. He offered it to whomever would decide to follow him. He knows we can't do it without his added help.

When I came to understand this, I took the final step. I told him that I was willing to leave my old way of life and to follow his new way if he would give me the strength needed to do it. I told him this out loud, as if he were in the room. I also invited him to enter my life and to forgive me of my previous way of living so we could begin to journey together. He accepted me without reservation and we began a new journey and a new life.

He offers you this same new life of embarking on a journey on a new road. If you don't feel confident in talking to God, but you want to take these three steps, the following is an example of what you could say to him.

Father God, I am in agreement with you that my deeds and ways of living have been wrong and I ask your forgiveness. I have come to believe that you Jesus, are the Son of God, and I invite you to enter my life. I have every intention of following you, but please give me the strength necessary to do it. Thank you for coming into my life in response to this prayer and for giving me eternal life.

The question is what happens after this petition to God? People usually have one of two reactions after this prayer. Some experience a sensation in their spirit of peace or joy or relief. Others don't sense anything special at all. That doesn't mean that nothing happened!

People in the first group experience a wide range of emotions. Personally, the moment I asked Jesus to enter my life and take control of it, I experienced the feeling of successfully resolving a difficult problem. I was relieved that the most important transaction of my life had been resolved; now I had God as a companion in life and the assurance of an eternal dwelling place with him. I experienced peace and went directly into a peaceful sleep. Some experience a sense of forgiveness and cleanness, others happiness.

For those in the second category who don't experience any special feelings, the following is an example that will interest you.

One evening my wife and I had invited some neighbors and friends to listen to a presentation on this theme of knowing God. After the presentation I gave those present an opportunity to take these three steps toward God. I gave them a sample prayer like the one above for those who would not know what to say. I encouraged them to just say it in their hearts and not out loud. After the meeting, a woman, a very close friend of ours, asked me if a person who said that prayer should feel anything special, some kind of emotion that would indicate Jesus had responded and had entered her life. It was evident she had taken those three steps without noting any special sensation.

I pointed her to some of the things Jesus had said on this subject. "Look! I have been standing at the door, and I am constantly knocking. If anyone hears me calling him and opens the door, I will come in and fellowship with him and he with me."[68]

There are three ideas in this saying of Jesus: the visitor, the homeowner, and the result. The visitor arrives at the door of one's heart or life and is calling to be invited in. We should note the visitor is knocking, waiting for the door to be opened. This is not a forced entry. Jesus respects your will. The second thing is the homeowner has a decision to make. Will he or she leave the visitor standing on the doorstep, hoping he will get tired and go away, or will he or she open the door and invite the visitor in?

In this saying of Jesus there is a promise, "If anyone hears me calling him and opens the door, I will come in." He promises to enter if invited. Our assurance of his entry depends on our confidence that he will perform what he said. We can't grab him by the arm and drag him in since he is spiritual and not physical. If we believe Jesus is a man of his word then we will have the confidence he has done what he said he would do. If we have done our part in inviting him in, he will do his part in coming in.

The lady I mentioned before had invited him into her life. Once she realized that despite her lack of any special feelings she could trust Jesus to do what he had promised, she returned home believing he had heard and responded to her. During the next few days her life was notably changed. It became evident to all that she was becoming a different person, one who was walking in the ways of Jesus. The love of God in her life became obvious to all. The evidence of the presence of Jesus in her was clear.

Some Benefits of This New Life

These changes are just the introduction to a new life. It is as if someone is a citizen of one country and becomes a citizen of another. Everything is new. The government is different, the customs, the people, and the ways of life.

The Bible was written in ancient times when most of the nations had a king to govern them. It uses the illustration of passing from one kingdom to another, and entering the kingdom of Jesus Christ. It is a spiritual kingdom, as Jesus said to Pilate, "My kingdom is not of this world."[69] He becomes the governing authority for those who receive him. He does not enter our lives to become our servant. He comes to be lord and ruler so that we do his will, not just what we want. However, he is not a hard taskmaster. He is a ruler who loves us profoundly and we will find that his will is good and acceptable to us.

He has never asked me to do anything bad or to harm another. He has always counseled to do good to my fellow man because he loves all people as much as he loves me. To make him ruler of my life means to live as he lived, loving everyone.

This new life is lived by new principles. Under my old principles, if lying was beneficial to me, I saw it as good. But this new life is different. God counsels me to stop all forms of deceit. There are better ways that bring better results. He is the lord of truth, not of deceit. If someone is sincerely following God's ways of truth, people he encounters discover they can trust what he says even if they are his enemies.

Jesus' true followers have compassion on people in need and help them. Their families discover this person is a peacemaker rather than someone who creates tension. This true follower will find himself or herself being transformed in his or her own life.

Bitterness leaves his or her life and is replaced increasingly by peace and tranquility. Day after day people around them observe the transformation that begins taking place as the "follower" experiences God's love in their own life. He or she not only has become a citizen of another kingdom but also experiences a transformation of his or her own being.

When a person begins to walk with Jesus Christ, listening to his voice and to his advice, he discovers a transforming power that comes from God. It would be sad indeed if this new Kingdom consisted only of new laws, good laws, but ones impossible to follow. But the person who allows Jesus to enter his life discovers a powerful and renovating Spirit that finds residence in him.

By his help we begin experiencing the new life he expects us to live. This new life is made possible because we pay attention to him and depend on his help to live it.

I think the following story of a friend of mine will help you understand what I am saying:

My name is Segundo (Number Two) Navaza. Even though it is a common name in Spain where I was born, it has been a heavy weight to bear all of my life. People have always made comments about it especially when I was a kid. They would say things like, "runner up isn't the best spot" "where is number one?" "ah, I see, silver medal, not the gold" etc. Comments like these would be made each time I was introduced to another for the first time. This continues to this day even though I now am 45 years old!

Let me start my story by telling you I never was a religious person. Most Spaniards were Catholics but I abandoned all pretense of religion in my teens. That is when I stopped going to church. I still had respect for religious things but was careful to maintain my distance. As a secular person I struggled to find a moral philosophy to live by but could never resolve this issue. Deep inside of me I knew that someday I would have to find a solution to my disturbed conscience and moral dilemma.

When I started attending college I became very interested in politics. It was a time of dictatorship in our country, that of Franco, the extreme right. As I got to know other students, I became familiar with communist groups who opposed Franco. There were a lot of different groups, some radical and some moderate. I had a very difficult time understanding the differences between these groups. However, what was happening was a growing sensation of shame and indignation over the fact that my country was the only Western European country living with a right wing dictatorship. Hate and resentment began growing in me toward people and toward our national history.

As I associated with both liberal and conservative leftists, I began to observe that, like the dictatorship, they manipulated people and grabbed for personal power. This became really evident to me when Franco died and a power struggle ensued between the many political parties. The very people I had admired for their selflessness and sacrifice in the communist circles began to reveal their true moti-

vation for personal gain and power. I watched as people shifted from one political party to another trying to find their ways. I ended up in a moderate socialist group.

I was finding that more and more we communists were getting farther and farther from our original Leninist principles of "The State and Revolution" the book that, without a doubt, had the most profound impact on my life. I had also been very much influenced by "Ten Days that Shook The World" by the American newspaperman, J. Reed, about the Bolshevik revolution.

As a consequence of the freedom our country began experiencing, we also began experiencing the comfortable life that came with the disappearance of fear and danger. We could emerge from the clandestine life we had lived for many years under an oppressive state. It seems like we didn't know how to live in the open without repression. We had lived so many years of gathering in groups to protest against the government and having the police come and disperse us with clubs and beatings. Many years of clandestine printing presses, illegal magazines, and secret meetings on dark streets and in homes to escape detection were now history.

In this new situation we began to experience moderation and change in our ideology since it was no longer illegal. Our ideal began to degenerate and we began to compromise our stand. We began to contradict ourselves and didn't know where we stood.

This resulted in an identity crisis for me. I had lost my political ideal. I tried covering this over with intense living and substituting other interests. I began to mix with people of other ideologies and viewpoints as they accepted me with mine. My curiosity led me to listen to other philosophies and ways of living to cover up my own internal moral conflict.

I began to party and my college studies grew less and less important to me as I searched for meaning to life. I began experimenting with drugs and soon I discovered I was becoming a nervous wreck. My life became an anguish day and night and I began to fear I would die. My life was a mess and I was trapped in it without any way out.

During this time, one of my friends, Ana, whom I thought a bit strange, told me of her experience with God that had transformed her. I laughed at her and began avoiding her when I saw her coming to or from class. At this time, my father, whom I admired very much, suddenly died of a heart attack. This forced me to temporarily leave college and to return home to be with my mother who had recently acquired a drug store. Although I did not drop out of college, I did spend most of my time for a couple of years trying to keep us out of debt and trying to make the business succeed.

Life permanently changed for me with the death of my father. The one person in whom I confided was gone. I became very insecure and needed treatment for anguish and anxiety. My psychologist more or less told me, "You don't really have anything wrong but you are suffering as if you had the worst sickness imaginable." Even with this, I continued with a heavy nightlife. One night after heavy drinking and smoking pot, my heartbeat sped up to 200 beats per minute. That night I promised myself I would turn over a new leaf. But the next night I was back to the old life.

When my father died, for whatever reason, there was only one person who wrote me and expressed her condolences and sympathy. Yes, you can imagine, it was Ana, the one who had spoken to me about Jesus Christ a year before. I didn't attach a lot of importance to it, but I remembered it. After that, once again we encountered each other near the campus and she invited me to get acquainted with "Christian people" camping during the summer.

Out of curiosity I joined them. It was here I saw people living out their Christianity. As we camped together I could observe their Christianity firsthand and I saw something I had never seen before anywhere. There were simple things like mutual respect, pure love, and a sincere interest in each other. I realized what I was observing was not put on; they really loved each other. I saw that if someone rubbed another the wrong way they solved the problem. They were not typical examples of religious people, but more like people experiencing freedom. What deeply impressed me was that they were truly free, free to joke around, to express love and concern, to converse on any subject freely.

One afternoon during our camping, just before playing soccer together, I prayed for the first time in my life. I looked up into the sky and said something similar to, Lord, if you can change my life,

I entrust it to you. I realize I have failed, now see what you can do with it.

I went out and played goalie for our side. They put some goals in but I didn't react as I normally would have. A few hours after the game I realized I was a different person. I didn't let anyone know of my decision until the next day because I wasn't sure how real the change was. I discovered I was staying well beyond the amount of days that I had planned to stay. Something extraordinary was happening to me, it was a mixture of peace I had never known before, and at the same time joy. All of my experiences up to that point I saw as ridiculous and artificial compared to what I was now experiencing. Finally, I couldn't keep quiet anymore and I told everyone I had converted to Jesus Christ. Of course, they were excited for me.

As I returned to my town of a population of about 5,000, I faced the prospect of living this new life at home among friends and relatives. My town was a town of unbelieving people; I may have been the only Christian among them. It wasn't long before I realized half the town had learned of my new life with Christ and people talked about it all of the time. Most of them couldn't understand what had happened to me. Soon I found that people I used to hate, those with the opposite political view, I didn't hate any longer. In fact, I found I loved them without reservation.

The person who was especially taken by surprise by the changes in me was my mother. She observed that as soon as I got home from the camping trip I stopped running around at night and was enjoying being with her and watching television together, something we had never done before. She was taken by surprise and wondered why I had stopped my nocturnal life. She could hardly believe I was regularly helping out with the drug store.

We had opened this drug store just one month before my father died. We had borrowed a lot of money to get it going so for a few months the financial pressure was pretty heavy. We had never done very well being in debt, and owing the bank was very draining emotionally for my mother and me.

To our great surprise, the month following my return from camping, all of our debt was eliminated, as the drug store became a great success. This was a sign from heaven for me, since for a number of years we had been running in the red in our family finances.

My life changed so radically that my mother, who had been very religious but without God, began to search for him. Today she knows and experiences God in the same way I do.

My life with Jesus Christ was an enormous change from my prior life as I experienced his sufficiency and power. Love, joy and an extraordinary peace were my daily experience and my only desire was to tell everyone I knew about it. This surprised me because I had always been an introvert. At our political gatherings I never spoke publicly as it totally embarrassed me. Now I spoke freely without fear. The fear of death I had lived with before was gone and now I saw death as something normal, not terrible.

The most surprising thing was I no longer had a nervous condition, rapid heartbeat, or anguish. They were completely gone. For some reason it totally surprised me that though I didn't have any other Christian acquaintances, I was experiencing the full range of this joy and peace. I kept available a New Testament they had given to me, read it and talked to God daily. I had surprising strength of spirit and easily endured the misunderstanding and ridicule that many heaped upon me. Without a doubt God had come into my life and I valued it enormously.

Since then, Jesus Christ has filled the empty parts of my life. In the light of the Scriptures, I understood this total peace was a result of the forgiveness I had received when I talked to God that day out camping. The joy I was experiencing was the discovery of a new life, a life I now could live with God as my friend.

I knew that this was not temporary. I needed to continue discovering more and more things about this new life. I had discovered what I had always wanted without knowing it or what it was called. It was God. It had to be God.

As the years have passed I have been learning more and more about the God who made himself known to me out in that place of nature, the field and the forest where we played soccer. I keep learning about him and continue desiring to know more about him. I continue to believe there can be no other life so special, so abundant, as the life that Jesus Christ gives.

The New Life Has Its Difficult Side, Too

Jesus is honest with us. He said that this new life is a good life but is also difficult at times. He promises his presence and help when the storms of life come upon us. He will not keep us from these storms, or difficult circumstances in life, but does promise to help us through them.

Sometimes we go through periods of a lack of confidence in him as we face internal and external problems. Possibly you have been an alcoholic or drug addict or have some other addiction. He offers his power to become liberated from addictions or other problems but there come times when we neglect to take advantage of his help. We can fall back into our old habits. We should not lose hope. He never abandons those who receive and follow Christ. He always offers us new hope and help to overcome what has chained us.

Other difficult situations such as the death of a loved one or bad health come upon all of us at one time or another. Or maybe people near you reject or oppose your new faith. He warns us that difficult times will come. So we may expect delays, pain, problems, and difficulties. We may also expect his presence, his comfort, his help, his counsel, and his wisdom.

Our sufferings do not compare with the benefits he gives us. He uses all of these difficulties for our benefit. Amazing! He is wise, compassionate and powerful. Life with him is an amazing adventure. I have been walking this life for over forty years and would not exchange it for anything. There is nothing comparable.

I would like to leave you with three quotes from God in the Bible that sum up this new life.

"But the fruit of the Spirit is love, joy, peace, patience, kindness, goodness, faithfulness, gentleness and self-control."[70]

"Then he said to them all: 'If anyone would come after me, he must deny himself and take up his cross daily and follow me.'"[71]

"… God has said, 'Never will I leave you; never will I forsake you.'"[72]

For anyone reading this book who has encountered God, I want to encourage you to keep seeking to know more of what he is like, and keep finding out more of how to live this new life by regularly reading the Bible. Start in the New Testament. It is where we find the accounts of the life, thoughts, and acts of Jesus. God will speak to you through it and will guide you in your journey through life.

For the person who still has plenty of doubts, I recommend for you the path I used to work my way through my doubts. Read the New Testament with an open mind and consider this amazing person, Jesus. Keep asking yourself, "Who is this man?" Don't give up: the search is worth the treasure you will find! God himself said, "You will seek me and find me when you seek me with all your heart."[73]

Endnotes

[1] John 8:39,40. (The Bible) NIV

[2] John 4:24 KVJ

[3] Ankerberg and Weldon, *Darwin's Leap of Faith*, Eugene, Harvest House Publishers, 1998, p. 212 citing Stephen Jay Gould, *The Return of Hopeful Monsters*, Natural History, June-July 1997, p. 22.

[4] Lipson, H.S. *A Physicist Looks at Evolution*, Physics Bulletin, Vol. 31, 1980, p. 138.

[5] Ankerberg and Weldon, *Darwin's Leap of Faith*, Eugene, Harvest House Publishers, 1998, pp. 187,188 citing Coppedge, *Evolution: Possible or Impossible?*, Grand Rapids: Zondervan, 1973, p. 114.

[6] Ankerberg and Weldon, *Darwin's Leap of Faith*, Eugene, Harvest House Publishers, 1998, p.198.

[7] Huse, Scott M., *The Collapse of Evolution*, Grand Rapids, Baker Books, 1996, pp. 31-32.

[8] Huse, Scott M., *The Collapse of Evolution*, Grand Rapids, Baker Books, 1997, pp. 49-50.

[9] Denton, Michael, *Evolution: A Theory in Crisis,* Bethesda, Adler and Adler Publishers, 1985, p.234.

[10] Ibid., pp. 238-239.

[11] McDowell, Josh, *The New Evidence That Demands A Verdict,* Thomas Nelson, Inc. Publishers, 1999, p. 376.

[12] Genesis 14:8 NIV.

[13] 1 Kings 10:29 NIV.

[14] Judges 20:15, 16, NIV.

[15] McDowell, Josh, *The New Evidence That Demands A Verdict,* Thomas Nelson, Inc. Publishers, 1999, p. 380.

[16] Ibid. p.74, quotes Davidson, Samuel, *Hebrew Text of the Old Testament,* London, 1856, p 89.

[17] Ibid., pp. 74, 75, quotes Kenyon, Frederic, *Our Bible and the Ancient Manuscripts,* London, Eyre and Spottiswoode, 1939, p. 43.

[18] Ibid., p. 78, quotes Earle, Ralph, *How We Got Our Bible,* Grand Rapids: Baker Book House, 1971, pp. 48,49.

[19] Ibid, pp. 78.

[20] Ibid., p. 34, Geisler, Norman L. and William E. Nix, *A General Introduction to the Bible,* Chicago: Moody Press, 1986, p. 385.

[21] Ibid., p. 34, Leach, Charles, *Our Bible, How We Got It,* Chicago, Moody Press, 1898, p. 145.

[22] Ibid., p. 35, Kenyon, Frederic G., *Handbook to the Textual Criticism of the New Testament,* London, Macmillan and Company, 1901, p.4.

[23] Ibid., pp. 36, 37,quotes Bruce, F.F., *The New Testament Documents: Are They Reliable?* Downers Grove, Ill. InterVarsity Press, 1964, pp.16,17.

[24] John 10:31-33, NIV.

[25] John 5:18. NIV.

[26] Matthew 2:1-5. NIV.

[27] Micah 5:2, NASB.

[28] Isaiah 7:14, NIV.

[29] Isaiah 9:6, NIV.

[30] John 6:38, NIV.

[31] Ibid., 17:5.

[32] Ibid., 1:1,14.
[33] Ibid., 20:24-28.
[34] Morison, Frank, *Who Moved The Stone?*, Lamplighter Books, Zondervan Publishing House, Grand Rapids, Mi., 1976.
[35] Ibid., pg 11.
[36] Matthew 8:23-27, NIV.
[37] Mark 11:12-14, 20-21, NIV.
[38] Luke 7:11-16, NIV.
[39] John 11:1-3. NIV.
[40] Ibid., 11:17-45.
[41] Ibid., 2:1-11.
[42] Mark 2:4-12. NIV.
[43] John 10:18, NIV.
[44] Matthew 28:18,19, NIV.
[45] Acts 1:9, NIV.
[46] 1 Corinthians 15:4-8. NASB.
[47] John 13:35, NIV.
[48] Philippians 4:6,7, NIV.
[49] John 16:24, NIV.
[50] John 4:47-53, NIV.
[51] Titus 3:5, NIV.
[52] 1 John 1:9, NIV.
[53] Isaiah 1:18, NIV.
[54] Hebrews 13:5.
[55] John 16:24. NIV.
[56] Goforth, Rosalind, *How I Know God Answers Prayer*, Bethel Publishing, Elkhart, IN.
[57] Romans 8:32, NIV.
[58] 1 John 5:11-12, NIV.
[59] Revelation 3:20, NIV.
[60] 1 Thessalonians 5:9,10, (TLB).
[61] Luke 19:2-10. NASB.
[62] Luke 19:9-10, NIV.
[63] John 4:4-42, NASB.
[64] John 4:23, NIV.
[65] John 3

[66] Mark 10:17-27.
[67] John 8:12, NIV.
[68] Revelation 3:20, (TLB).
[69] John 18:36, NIV.
[70] Galatians 5:22,23, NIV.
[71] Luke 9:23, NIV.
[72] Hebrews 13:5, NIV.
[73] Jeremiah 29:13, NIV.

CPSIA information can be obtained
at www.ICGtesting.com
Printed in the USA
FSOW01n0141210417
33373FS